ABRAHAM
LINCOLN

POCKET
GIANTS

For Rosie, Eleanor & Lucy

ABRAHAM LINCOLN

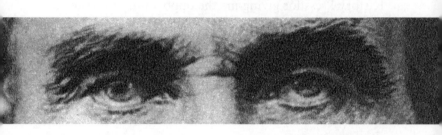

POCKET
GIANTS

ADAM I.P. SMITH

Acknowledgements

Thank you to Richard Carwardine, David Sim, Daniel Peart and Graham Peck, and my editor Tony Morris, all of whom read the text and made wise suggestions. I am grateful to The History Press for giving me the opportunity to write 'my' Lincoln in a form that was highly congenial to me.

Cover image © Mary Evans Picture Library

First published 2014

The History Press
The Mill, Brimscombe Port
Stroud, Gloucestershire, GL5 2QG
www.thehistorypress.co.uk

© Adam I.P. Smith, 2014

The right of Adam I.P. Smith to be identified as the Author of this work has been asserted in accordance with the Copyright, Designs and Patents Act 1988.

British Library Cataloguing in Publication Data.
A catalogue record for this book is available from the British Library.

ISBN 978 0 7524 9775 4

Typesetting and origination by The History Press
Printed in Malta by Gutenberg Press Ltd.

Contents

1

'Who Was Abraham Lincoln?'

His structure was loose and leathery; his body was shrunk and shrivelled; he had dark skin, dark hair, and looked woe-struck ... His walk was undulatory – catching and pocketing time, weariness and pain, all up and down his person, and thus preventing them from locating.

Herndon, William & Weik, Jesse W., *Herndon's Lincoln*, Wilson, Douglas L. & Davis, Rodney O. (eds) (University of Illinois Press, 2006), p. 351

Leo Tolstoy was a great teller of tales. 'Once while travelling in the Caucuses,' he told a reporter from the *New York World* in 1909, he happened to be the guest of a tribal chief, 'who, living far away from civilized life in the mountains, had but a fragmentary and childish comprehension of the world and its history. The fingers of civilization had never reached him nor his tribe, and all life beyond his native valleys was a dark mystery.' Gathering his sons and neighbours around him – a 'score of wild looking riders … sons of the wilderness' – the chief asked Tolstoy to tell them about the great men of the world. 'I spoke at first,' recalled Tolstoy, 'of our Czars and their victories; then I spoke of the greatest military leaders. My talk seemed to impress them greatly. The story of Napoleon was so interesting to them that I had to tell them every detail, as, for instance, how his hands looked, how tall he was, who made his guns and pistols and the colour of his horse.' Yet this was not enough. 'But you have not told us a syllable about the greatest general and greatest ruler of the world,' said the chief gravely. 'We want to know something about him. He was a hero. He spoke with a voice of thunder; he laughed like the sunrise and his deeds were as strong as the rock and as sweet as the fragrance of roses. The angels appeared to his mother and predicted that the son whom she would conceive would become the greatest the stars had ever seen. He was so great that he even forgave the crimes of his greatest enemies and shook brotherly hands with those who had plotted against his life. His name was Lincoln and the country in which he lived is called America, which is so far away that if a youth should journey to reach it he would be an old man when he arrived. Tell us of that man.'[1]

What are we to make of this story? Why did it sound plausible to people who read it? First, it reminds us that Lincoln's image has transcended the historical reality of the flesh-and-blood man. He matters to us today almost as much for what his image has come to mean as for what he achieved in his lifetime. Second, Tolstoy's story is evidence that Lincoln – in so many ways the quintessential American figure – is also a global figure. The America Lincoln represents is universal: a place and an idea that matters to non-Americans as well. He embodies a 'good' America, defined in opposition to its imperialism or materialism. It was, after all, Lincoln who spoke about his struggle to defeat the Confederacy in the Civil War as the battle to ensure that 'government of the people, by the people, for the people shall not perish from the earth'.[2] For him, as for most other Americans in the nineteenth century – and many others around the world – it was literally true that the United States was the 'last, best hope of earth'.[3]

Tolstoy's Lincoln story suggests that Lincoln has been a figure in world history not just because of what he did but also because of what, or who, he seems to be. This brings us to a paradox. For all that has been written about Lincoln, he remains somehow unknowable. The facts of his life are clear enough. We have an eight-volume set of his writings and thousands of items of incoming correspondence, freely searchable on the Library of Congress website. His face is chiselled into Mount Rushmore; it is on the 1¢ coin and the $5 bill. He is famous enough to have featured in *The Simpsons*, in a film about vampire slayers and even in the *National Enquirer* (in a story claiming he was a cross-dresser). We feel we should know Lincoln; yet, like colleagues and associates in his own lifetime, in many important ways we don't. William Herndon, who spent the best part of ten years sharing a law office with him, thought Lincoln one of the most 'shut-mouthed men' he had ever met when it came to his inner thoughts. In fact, apart from his combustible relationship with his wife Mary, Lincoln really only ever had one truly close friend, Joshua Speed. And even that friendship became more distant after both had married. (Speed ended up running a slave plantation in Kentucky when his old friend rose to the leadership of the new antislavery party, the Republicans.)

Tolstoy told all he knew, but his listeners wanted more. The great novelist promised to ride to the nearest town to find them a photograph. Sometime later he returned and presented the portrait of Lincoln to one of the tribesmen, whose 'hands trembled' as he 'gazed for several minutes silently like one in a reverent prayer'. 'Don't you find,' said the tribesman after a while, 'judging from his picture, that his eyes are full of tears and that his lips are sad with a secret sorrow?' Lincoln's mournful eyes are indeed compelling. There was 'a strong tinge of sadness in Mr Lincolns composition', recalled a fellow lawyer. 'He felt very strongly that there was more of discomfort than real happiness in human existence [even] under the most favorable circumstances.'[4]

Lincoln suffered from bouts of depression throughout his life. He once confessed that he sought company because when he was by himself he could be so overwhelmed with sadness that he 'never dare[d] carry a knife in his pocket'.[5] His melancholy was well known among those who knew him. People saw it not as an illness but as a natural way of being and one that was associated with exceptional talent. Romantic poets, after all, were the heroes of Lincoln's age. Rather than a weakness, a thoughtful, reflective sadness could be a sign of depth and manliness. Civil War soldiers not only routinely slept cuddled up together ('spooning', they called it), but also sang sentimental songs with titles like 'Weeping Sad and Lonely' and no one questioned their manhood for doing so.

To his poet-biographer Carl Sandburg, one source of Lincoln's fascination was his contrasting qualities. He was 'steel and velvet … hard as rock and soft as drifting fog'. The man who broke down in tears in front of a press reporter and a senator, after hearing that the dashing young Elmer Ellsworth, his former law clerk, had been shot by a rebel sympathiser in May 1861, was also the man who refused to visit his dying father despite the desperate pleas of his stepbrother.[6] There are many Lincolns – many people who claim him as their own. In Lincoln's 'ordinariness' is not just a familiar humanity, but the tantalising glimpse of his vulnerability.

Ultimately, however, Abraham Lincoln qualifies as a historical 'giant' not because of the ways his image and the stories about him have drawn so many to him, but quite simply because he was at the centre of events that shaped the modern world. His election to the presidency of the United States in 1860 was such a provocation to the southern slave-holding states that eleven of them carried out a long-standing threat to break away from the Union, forming a separate, independent Confederacy. It was Lincoln as much as anyone who was willing to use violence in response to the break-up of the United States. Herndon remembered Lincoln, as President-Elect, vowing to 'make one vast grave yard of the valley of the Mississippi – yes of the whole South, if I must – to maintain, preserve, and defend the Union and Constitution in all their ancient integrity'.[7] Such words were cheap before the first shot had been fired; there followed a four-year civil war that, as is the case with most conflicts, cost far more in blood and treasure than anyone foresaw. At least 670,000 people had been killed by the time General Lee surrendered at Appomattox on Palm Sunday 1865. To Lincoln's supporters these were sacrifices made on the altar of the nation.

Through his words as well as his actions – for his elegant, unpretentious prose makes him one of the world's greatest political speechwriters – Lincoln is imagined as having 're-founded' the American nation. If George Washington brought what he called the 'great experiment' of the new republic into being, it was Lincoln who defined it and secured its future – and thus laid the foundations for the United States' twentieth-century dominance. Lincoln's nationalism has worn well historically because he offered a liberal, antislavery vision of the nation that seems modern. He may appear a slightly comical figure in modern popular culture, with his absurdly tall hat and an arrangement of facial hair that has never since been fashionable, yet he is also a relevant one, for with only a little imagination, Lincoln's political sensibility appears not so distant from our own. Today, he is claimed by liberals as well as by conservatives, and held up by virtually all as a yardstick against whom the pygmy politicians of the present are measured.

Lincoln's perceived relevance – his place in the historical imagination of generations of people in the United States and beyond – also owes much to his role in the abolition of slavery. More than 4 million people of African ancestry were emancipated during or immediately after the American Civil War, although their future legal status in the United States remained unclear at the time of Lincoln's death. The Confederacy had claimed its place alongside the multiple other nationalities emerging in the mid-nineteenth century despite, or even because of, its assertion that a particular race of human beings could be bought and sold like property. This coerced human property was the basis of the South's economy. How might industrial capitalism have developed differently had the South won? We will never know, but the potential weight of the question indicates why northern victory seemed at the time, and ever since, to have mattered so much. If Lincoln does not necessarily deserve as much credit as he has sometimes received for the abolition of slavery, he certainly played the principal role in binding emancipation into a compelling narrative of the meaning of the war. To a remarkable extent, the dominant interpretation of the Civil War is Lincoln's. It was he who wanted people to see Union victory as a triumph of modernity (though southern slaveholders were nothing if not modern in their own way – operating as fully fledged capitalists in a global market). It was Lincoln, too, who, above all, wanted people to associate the United States with freedom and to see that its use of force was for the universal benefit of mankind. When we talk about Lincoln, we are reckoning with both the historical man and his legacy.

The Civil War is not just the formative story of American nationhood, nor did it matter only as the most dramatic chapter in the story of emancipation and economic development. It was also a central event in the nineteenth century. It disrupted world trade and polarised politics as far afield as Brazil and Britain. At stake in the conflict seemed to be all the issues that were coursing through the world at this moment of heightened global inter-connectedness: what was a nation? Could democracy replace older forms of authority? What, in practice, did 'freedom' mean? Abraham Lincoln was at the centre of it all.

The United States mattered to Europeans in the nineteenth century as a promise (or, to some, a threat) of the possibility of popular government. Many of the leading political thinkers of the time understood the great question of the age as being about the struggle for democratic nationhood – that is, states defined by and responsive to 'the people' rather than barons, kings, or emperors. In this dichotomous world, Lincoln came to represent democracy more perfectly than any other figure, not just because of what he said or did, but because of who he was. Narratives of Lincoln's life were published regularly in Europe as well as America in the late nineteenth and early twentieth centuries, and at their core was the story of his rise from humble origins to the highest office in the land – from the 'plough to the presidency', as one British biographer put it.[8]

What put the seal on the Lincoln legend was his assassination, on Good Friday, 14 April 1865. The President had been in unusually good spirits that day, telling some of his Cabinet members about a dream that he believed augured good fortune. The war was over. General Lee, the Confederate commander, had surrendered and his bedraggled, hungry men appeared only too willing to disband and trek back to their homes. That evening, Lincoln and his wife Mary rode by carriage from the White House to Ford's Theatre for a performance of a popular British comedy. The Lincolns were late, missing the first few minutes of the play. The action on stage stopped as they appeared in a box to take their seats and the band struck up 'Hail to the Chief'. Waiting for Lincoln that night was a well-known actor and Confederate sympathiser, John Wilkes Booth. This was Wilkes' moment on the world stage, with himself as the hero of a melodrama of revenge and catharsis. '*Sic Semper Tyranis*' ('Thus, always to tyrants') some in the audience remembered Booth shouting as he jumped to the stage after shooting the President in the back of the head. Lincoln did not die at once, but he never regained consciousness. He was carried across the road to the ground-floor bedroom of a boarding house, where his life slipped away the following morning.

The news of Abraham Lincoln's assassination reached Europe twelve days later, at the speed of the fastest steamer. From Caen, in Normandy, came a resolution addressed to the American minister in Paris: 'Tell [your people] … that humanity has never given birth but in sorrow; that to just and holy causes there is need of noble martyrs, and that for the ages, the only true crowns are the crowns of thorns shining over Calvaries!' This was not the first, and it certainly wouldn't be the last, comparison of Lincoln with Christ. The words of the 'Battle Hymn of the Republic', written three years earlier by the abolitionist Julia Ward Howe, seemed to endow his death with providential meaning: 'as He died to make us holy, let us die to make men free.'

'Who was Abraham Lincoln that so much lamentation should be evoked by his death?' asked an English newspaper in May 1865.[9] It was the question the Caucasian chief asked Tolstoy and it is the question of this book.

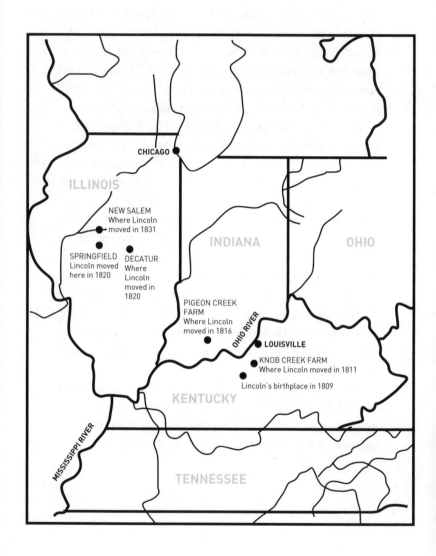

CHICAGO

ILLINOIS

NEW SALEM
Where Lincoln
moved in 1831

INDIANA

OHIO

SPRINGFIELD
Lincoln moved
here in 1820

DECATUR
Where
Lincoln
moved in
1820

PIGEON CREEK
FARM
Where Lincoln
moved in 1816

OHIO RIVER

LOUISVILLE

KNOB CREEK FARM
Where Lincoln moved in 1811

Lincoln's birthplace in 1809

KENTUCKY

MISSISSIPPI RIVER

TENNESSEE

Pioneer

'The short and simple annals of the poor.' That's my life, and that's all you or any one else can make of it.

Abraham Lincoln, *HI*, p. 57

Lincoln was born on 12 February 1809, in a log cabin in Hardin County, Kentucky, some 20 miles south of the broad bends of the Ohio River and on the edges of white settlement on the North American continent. His father, Thomas Lincoln, and his mother, Nancy Hanks, made a hard-won living from farming and wintertime carpentry, relying for food and clothing on what they could produce, hunt or barter. In 1816, after a dispute over land titles had deprived Thomas of much of what he thought he owned, he moved his family north of the Ohio River – then the border between states where slavery was legal and those where it was banned – to Pigeon Creek in Indiana. The young Abraham helped his father clear the forest, splitting logs for rail fences, ploughing fields by hand and building a rough cabin. Like other pioneer settlers, the Lincolns 'squatted' without rent on the land for a year before making a payment to the local branch of the Federal government land office. Lincoln later recalled Pigeon Creek as a 'wild region, with many bears and other wild animals still in the woods'.[10] It was there, when Abraham was 9, that his mother died of what folks at the time called 'milk sickness'. This tragedy was an all too familiar story in a society where a quarter of all children lost a parent in childhood. Lincoln was born into a world in which life was profoundly shaped by the elements: crops that sometimes failed, harsh winters, summer droughts and the arbitrariness of disease and sickness. And it was shaped also by the fatefulness of individual decisions about when and where to plant seeds, by the precariousness of law and order, and by thoughts about whether to heed the latest rumours of more fertile land that could be acquired cheaply somewhere else.

In the first twenty years of Lincoln's life the population of the United States almost doubled from 7 to 13 million. It was a dynamic society with a strongly egalitarian ethos among white men and a restless optimism about the possibility of improvement and progress. For common people on the frontier like the Lincolns it was also a rude and rough existence in which, despite the efforts of circuit-riding preachers and earnest middle-class reformers, drinking, swearing and violence were staple elements of a highly masculine culture. The Lincolns' Kentucky and Indiana must have felt very far from the sophisticated urban centres of the East Coast. To have travelled from Hardin County to New York City around the time the future President was born would have taken two or three months. Even after the opening of the Erie Canal in 1825 removed the need to trek through the Appalachian Mountains, the journey still took at least three or four weeks. Distance, poor roads and very little access to cash or credit meant that small-scale farmers like the Lincolns had few opportunities to sell any surplus produce to market. The most practical way to do it was to hand-build a flatboat and steer the crops down the Mississippi River to New Orleans, from where they could be shipped to New York, Boston or Philadelphia. The young Lincoln was hired to do this on two occasions. The journey downstream took several weeks and required both navigational skill and physical toughness to fight off opportunist thieves. And once the port of New Orleans was reached – a bustling cosmopolitan, multilingual city where slaves mingled with European sailors – and the goods had been sold, the only practical way home was to walk.

In later life, Lincoln was deeply ambivalent about the world in which he grew up. On the one hand, much of his young adulthood was spent finding a route out of the life his family led. His relationship with his father, which was never close, grew ever more strained. His beloved older sister died in childbirth aged 18. And once he had established himself as a middle-class professional, he penned some scolding letters to his stepbrother, John D. Johnston, criticising him for wanting to move west, as Lincoln's own parents had done. 'Squirming & crawling about from place to place can do no good,' Lincoln chastised, with evident feeling. Yet on the other hand, he was acutely aware of the political advantages of having worked his way to the top. His background provided him with a fount of rustic frontier anecdotes, which reinforced his air of sincerity and made him appear grounded. As President he in turns exasperated, confused and charmed those who met him with stories about chickens, hogs or drunken preachers, the immediate point of which was not always evident. His election campaigns made much of his humble origins – he was 'Honest Abe', the 'rail-splitter' whose folksy manner was a sign that he would be a new broom, sweeping away the corruption of the out-of-touch Washington political elite. Simultaneously romanticising as well as distancing himself from his early life, he told a campaign biographer in 1860 that his youth could be summed up in a 'single sentence, and that sentence you will find in Gray's *Elegy* – "The short and simple annals of the poor." That's my life, and that's all you or anyone else can make of it.'[11]

In 1819, Thomas Lincoln remarried. His new wife, Sarah Bush Johnston, arrived in Pigeon Creek with three precious books. She may well have played a role in encouraging Abraham's interest in a world beyond the farm. It must have been hard, nonetheless, for the teenage Lincoln to imagine a path in life for himself beyond the pioneer world of his family and neighbours. As was common practice on the frontier, families exchanged labour with one another, which meant that the young Lincoln did not just work on his own family's farm, but for neighbours as well. Occasionally Lincoln saw the direct fruits of his labour when a neighbour paid him in cash, but that was rare. Some historians have speculated that being tied into a family economy like this, with only minimal control of his own labour while he remained under his father's roof, may have provided the psychological origins of Lincoln's dislike of slavery: in his youth, he felt like a slave.[12] It's an intriguing notion but there is no evidence to support it, and in fact Lincoln remained with his family for longer than he needed. In 1830, Thomas Lincoln moved the family again, this time to central Illinois and, although

Lincoln was 'of age', he chose to accompany them. Not until he was 22 did Abraham leave his father's farm and set out to make his way independently in life.

It was then that he settled in the village of New Salem on the Sangamon River, about 15 miles north-west of Springfield. Rejecting the life of near-subsistence farming, the move, on his own, to New Salem was a bold one. He chose to define himself not by his family ('I have no wealthy or popular relations to recommend me,' he wrote), but by his own charisma.[13] His ability to make people laugh with amusing, sometimes ribald anecdotes, eased him into male company in particular. Older members of the community took him under their wings and he became known for his willingness to work hard and his honesty.

He tried his hand at store keeping (the store went bankrupt – 'winked out' as he put it – and Lincoln spent twenty years paying off the debt) and at surveying (an important job in a world of unsettled land with disputed titles). Eventually, he secured a (very part-time) position as the local postmaster, a Federal patronage post that gave him not only a regular income but also access to state and national newspapers. He was unusually tall at 6 foot 4 inches (an astonishing 8 inches taller than the average American man of his time), and years of farm labour had made him strong. One of his neighbours remembered him as a 'sort of monstrosity. His frame was large, long, bony and muscular – his head disproportionately small.'[14] His legs were long and his feet large, but his most remarkable feature was his arms: 'when standing straight, and letting his arms fall down his Sides, the points of his fingers would touch a point lower on his legs by nearly three inches than was usual with other persons.'[15] His physical strength served him well. Challenged to a fight because of an imagined slight by Jack Armstrong, a 'square built' man, 'strong as an ox', Lincoln held his own, and thereafter won the respect – and, handily, the votes and political support when he needed them – of Armstrong's gang of young men known as the Clary Grove Boys.[16] The mark of the esteem in which he was held by the other young men of New Salem was that in 1832 he won his first election: as captain of a militia company that set off to fight the Sac and Fox Native Americans in the Black Hawk War – a success, he later recalled, which 'gave me more pleasure than any I have had since'.[17] He thrived in a physically robust male environment despite rarely drinking hard liquor: it made him feel, he said, 'flabby and undone'. Though he sometimes took a drink, he was never drunk.[18] Perhaps the loss of self-control frightened him.

Physically imposing as he was, Lincoln's real prowess was as a talker. In New Salem, he became a leading member of the local young men's debating society. Male debating clubs, or Lyceums, were common even in the smallest settlements. They provided a school for oratorical skill and wit while also imbuing young men with patriotic values; a typical debate topic was, 'Resolved that Washington deserves more credit for defending his country than Columbus for discovering America'. For Lincoln, the New Salem debating society was his first taste of public speechmaking apart from the impromptu mimicry of local preachers with which he'd entertained his Indiana friends. At his first appearance in the New Salem debating club, he astonished his audience with his eloquence and powers of reasoning since 'all had anticipated the relation of some humorous story'.[19] Humour had a vital function: his stories, he once said, gave vent to his moods and gloom.[20] But public life was, for Lincoln, fundamentally a serious, purposeful business. And politics was where he chose to expend his considerable energy.

His fascination with politics did not in itself mark him out as unusual. When he turned 21, Lincoln, like all white men in Illinois, propertyless though he was, could vote and hold office. Compared to later and earlier periods in American history, there were remarkably few barriers to participation in politics, especially in the frontier West. Of course, money was useful, as were connections, but organisation and charisma could take a man a long way. Elections and campaigns were community events that were probably harder to avoid than to take part in. And political success, it turned out, was aided by attributes that Lincoln had in abundance: the ability to hold an audience of men and to earn their respect. At the age of 23, just a year after setting out to make his own way in the world, Lincoln ran for election to the Illinois state legislature. He did not win, lacking name recognition in many parts of the large district, but the evidence that he had found an outlet that suited his talents was that he polled more than 90 per cent of the vote in the township of New Salem where he was known. In electoral success, Lincoln found personal validation and an outlet for his growing ambition.

The huckstering yet high-minded world of politics offered an exciting route out of the ordinary paths in life. But at the same time, it seemed to matter because it offered a chance to shape his society in the direction he was already shaping himself. Lincoln's first election address, published in a local newspaper, expressed support for works to improve trade links and communications, 'commensurate with our infant resources'. He explained knowledgeably how the Sangamon River could be made more navigable and expressed support for better education and for regulation to control the rates of interest, a measure that would make credit more accessible in a cash-starved economy. These measures, Lincoln believed, would help clear the barriers to prosperity for ordinary men and women. At the level of a town like New Salem, national political issues (should there be a Bank of the United States?) seemed relevant because they appeared to be connected to similar local questions: how could farmers or businessmen get credit to invest? Should taxes be levied to pay for improved communications?

In the first twenty years of his public life, Lincoln talked about banking more than slavery; the availability of credit was to him more pressing an issue than the existence, south of the Ohio River, of humans held as property. But these seemingly pragmatic questions were in turn a reflection of a deeper, ideological one: how best to protect the freedom of 'the people' to succeed in what Lincoln called 'the race of life'? How to prevent monopolies of power, concentrations of wealth or tyrannical impulses from subverting the republic?

Election addresses to the 'independent voters', as Lincoln noted, were an 'established custom'. Not many, however, were written with the directness and apparent frankness of the 23-year-old Lincoln's: 'Every man is said to have his peculiar ambition,' Lincoln admitted. 'Whether it be true or not, I can say for one that I have no other so great as that of being truly esteemed by my fellow men, by rendering myself worthy of their esteem. How far I shall succeed in gratifying this ambition, is yet to be developed.'[21] Two years later, he ran again and this time, with better organisation and a longer campaign, he won decisively and took up his seat in the state's part-time legislature.

Lincoln came to political consciousness, and started down his own path to elected office, in an era in which by far the most dominant political personality on the national stage was President Andrew Jackson. 'Old Hickory', as he was known, was born in a North Carolina log cabin, was a military victor over the British in the war of 1812, an Indian-killer, duellist and Tennessee slaveholder. Jackson had first been elected in 1828 when Lincoln was 19, served two full terms in the White House and was then succeeded by his Vice President. Nathaniel Grigsby, one of Lincoln's boyhood friends from Indiana, recalled that in the 1820s, 'we were all Jackson boys & men'. But Lincoln's apparent youthful Jacksonianism did not survive his move to New Salem. 'What changed Lincoln [politically],' Grisby confessed, 'I don't remember', but plausibly Lincoln's rejection of Jackson was part of his effort to work his way out of his childhood world.[22] The anti-Jacksonian Whigs, with their language of self-control, self-improvement, economic development and respectability represented what Lincoln wanted to be rather than where he had come from. But in becoming a Whig, Lincoln's path to office in Illinois became much harder because Democrats dominated on a local as well as a national level. 'The Democracy', as the Jacksonian party often described itself, claimed, like their hero Old Hickory, to embody 'the people' against 'aristocratic' elites. They typically opposed government spending on roads – or on Lincoln's particular passion of aiding river navigation – on the grounds that an active government might become a tyrannical government. As a result, Lincoln scorned, Democrats were maintaining barriers to the advancement of the ordinary people they claimed to represent.

As is so often the case when an era is dominated by a strong leader who shapes the political agenda in profound ways, Jackson's opponents learned almost as much from him as his friends. Lincoln's public persona, especially when he ran for President in 1860, uncannily resembled Jackson's in his western, rustic origins and supposedly straightforward, 'homely' qualities. Like Jackson, Lincoln made his mark in the world as a democratic hero – that is, he came to personify the idea of popular government, of self-rule. Nowhere in Europe, as commentators at the time never ceased to observe, could a man of such humble origins rise to the top without violence. When working men looked at his face in the hauntingly clear photographs produced during the Civil War, they saw, or thought they saw, one of their own. To some that was a source of inspiration, to others a cause for alarm.

3

Self-Made Man

Work, work, work, is the main thing.

Abraham Lincoln

From his own experience, Lincoln drew the lesson that self-discipline, individual initiative and hard work could bring rewards. To an aspiring lawyer who asked for advice, the by-then successful Lincoln responded: 'the mode is very simple, though laborious, and tedious. It is only to get the books, and read, and study them carefully … Work, work, work, is the main thing.'[23] That such individual effort would be rewarded was the great blessing of the American republic, Lincoln thought. When he talked about 'our government' he did not mean some distant state power, but a system of self-rule the genius of which was to 'elevate the condition of men – to lift artificial weights from all shoulders – to clear the paths of laudable pursuit for all'.[24]

Lincoln always included ignorance as one of the fetters that could hold men back. Education, he wrote in his first election address, was the 'most important subject which we as a people can be engaged in'. It was for society as a whole what it had been for him personally: nothing less than the means by which a community would achieve 'morality, sobriety, enterprise and industry'.[25] Although he had no formal education beyond the most basic instruction in literacy, Lincoln had, from an early age, read 'all the books he could lay his hands on' and was a 'constant reader' of newspapers.[26] A New Salem neighbour recalled that 'he could usually be seen with a book under his arm, or open in his hand reading as he walked'. And his range was wide: 'Arithmetic, then Natural philosophy, Astronomy & Chemistry, then Surveying, and Law ... History.' 'My mind,' Lincoln once said, 'is like a piece of steel, very hard to scratch any thing on it and almost impossible after you get it there to rub it out.'[27] By his early twenties he had committed to memory large chunks of Shakespeare, Byron, Milton, Burns and other poets, together with passages from Euclid, the philosopher Thomas Brown and the theologian William Paley. 'Intense thought was with him the rule and not as with most of us the exception,' recalled his friend Joshua Speed.[28]

Lincoln's doctrine of improvement – for the self and for society – was characteristic of his generation. It made sense in the context of the opportunities being opened up by a rapidly changing economy. Fittingly, the term 'self-made man' came into general usage at the time that Lincoln left his family to make his own way in the world. The man who popularised it was Henry Clay, a Whig politician from Kentucky who Lincoln called my 'beau-ideal of a statesman'.[29] Clay's 'self-made men' were the new class of small-scale capitalist entrepreneurs whose own unaided effort was creating national prosperity. Clay's vision of the American future, which Lincoln enthusiastically shared, was a nation of factories as well as farms, of ceaseless growth, in which all had a chance of success in the race of life. To have made oneself was not just about acquiring money, but also respectability. It was a cultural archetype that helped to justify and explain a potentially destabilising transition from a society based on families to one based on individual success. Celebrating entrepreneurialism and rootlessness, the idea of the self-made man emerged as rapidly expanding agricultural production created wealth, pushed up land values and created new white-collar opportunities such as in the expanding legal profession. Lincoln was the beneficiary of that transformation, and if anyone in nineteenth-century America came to personify the self-made ideal, it was him.

His father, Thomas, had lived in a world shaped by the need to survive from one winter to the next, in which men were dependent on extended networks of family and neighbours, and where money was a scarce – and scarcely necessary – commodity. Thomas has often been portrayed as a failure, even though within his own world he had been a successful pioneer farmer and family man, remembered as 'good, clean, social, truthful & honest'.[30] Abraham inherited his father's reputation for 'honesty', but his ambition for personal success drove him inexorably off the land and into a cash-based, individualistic, urbanising world quite alien to his father.

In 1837, Lincoln moved from New Salem to the new state capital of Springfield, having obtained his state licence as a lawyer, arriving with all his possessions in a couple of saddle bags. The law and politics went hand in hand in nineteenth-century America; most office holders were lawyers and the profession provided exactly the right training and opportunity to become widely known, which aided a political career. No college degree was necessary, only an apprenticeship and some persistence. A fellow

Whig legislator, John T. Stuart, spotted Lincoln's talent and became one of several important figures who served as sort of patrons, in Stuart's case by lending him a copy of Blackstone's *Commentaries on the Laws of England*, still the foundation text for early nineteenth-century American lawyers. Stuart later took Lincoln on as a law partner. As a frontier lawyer, Lincoln made a living riding the circuit, which, before the railroads came in the 1850s, meant literally riding, on horseback, from one tiny town courthouse to the next. A good lawyer – and Lincoln, it turned out, was a very good lawyer – needed to be quick-witted and to understand the people he was dealing with. He needed common sense.

After his death, Lincoln's time as a prairie lawyer was almost as romanticised as his 'rail-splitting' youth. From the beginning of his practice, recalled a fellow lawyer, he was 'distinguished for fairness and candor in conducting or defending suits, as well as for clear, Logical Statements and deductions'.[31] In the 1830s and 1840s, as he was establishing his reputation, he took whatever cases that presented themselves, including, on one occasion, representing a slaveholder who was suing in the courts for the return of his runway 'property'. By the 1850s, though, Lincoln was earning a significant amount of money as a railroad attorney – a reflection not only of his increasing professional success, but of the economic transformation of those decades.

Lincoln's ambition to make the most of himself in this changing economy demanded an outward self-confidence. As a raconteur or as a sage source of advice, he found it easy to gather a large circle of friends and admirers; he had mentors who saw promise in him and companions with whom he would swap stories and share books. But his outward shell of good humour concealed a darker, introspective and sometimes utterly despairing inner self. 'His melancholy,' wrote his later law partner William Herndon, 'dripped from him as he walked.'[32]

Having physically removed himself from the potentially close bonds of his extended family, Lincoln seemed to struggle to express strong emotions or form intimate relations. And on at least two occasions he suffered serious mental breakdowns, both seemingly triggered by heartbreak, or at least by being suddenly confronted with how emotionally attached he had allowed himself to become to another person. One such crisis followed the sickness and death of a young New Salem woman, Ann Rutledge. The story became a staple of Lincoln lore in the late nineteenth and early twentieth centuries. Ann, a 'quiet soft bud of a woman' or a 'slim girl with corn-silk hair', has often been presented as Lincoln's only true love.[33] The evidence for Lincoln's love for Ann are really inferences drawn from the severity of his depression after her death, which worried his New Salem friends so much that they, in effect, mounted a suicide watch.

A similar crisis occurred in Springfield a few years later when Joshua Speed, Lincoln's great friend, with whom he shared a room and a bed above a general store in Springfield, left to get married back in his home state of Kentucky. At about the same time – and it is unclear exactly how these two events were related – Lincoln broke off his own fraught engagement with Mary Todd, the well-born daughter of a Kentucky slaveholder who had prominent relatives in Springfield. 'I am now the most miserable man living,' Lincoln wrote at that time. 'If what I feel were equally distributed to the whole human family, there would not be one cheerful face on the earth. Whether I shall ever be better I can not tell; I awfully forebode that I shall not.'[34] Yet somehow, whether using humour or taking succour in a wry fatalism, Lincoln always found the resources to recover. With him, the blackest pessimism could be quickly followed by unbounded confidence. His thirst for political success seemed also to drive him through his depressions: Herndon described him as 'totally swallowed up in his ambitions' (though his ambitions, thought Herndon, were a mixture of 'selfishness' and 'nobility').[35]

A year after they broke up, Lincoln and Mary Todd resuscitated their romance and did, after all, get married – and marriage was truly a step into the unknown for Lincoln. Older women had often mothered him, but women of his own generation were a different matter. He may have visited prostitutes (as his friend Speed certainly did), but the implications of wedded domesticity may well have been terrifying, especially, perhaps, in light of the class threshold he was crossing in making a match with someone of Mary Todd's background. Mary had her own demons – she suffered from intense migraines and was herself prone to depression – but she was highly intelligent and could be breathtakingly charming in company. The nature of their subsequent life together has been the source of much speculation. Some saw them as a very oddly matched couple – the Kentucky belle, plump and diminutive, and the strange long-limbed lawyer. Lincoln's law partner and later biographer, William Herndon, thought their marriage was miserable and mounted an all-out assault on Mary's personality, calling her 'the female wild-cat of the age'. He claimed that Mary was frequently in such a rage that she hurled vegetables and blunt objects at her husband, driving him out to spend the night on the sofa in his law offices.[36] Yet with Mary, Lincoln built a stable, middle-class, domestic life of a kind that he had never known. Their marriage had passion and commitment as well as explosive rows. Mary fuelled the fires of Abraham's ambition, becoming a wise source of advice. She was as intelligent and interested in politics as he. She was probably also more sharp-edged and waspish: they had rekindled their courtship by writing scurrilous anonymous letters for the *Sangamo Journal* lampooning a Democratic office holder. 'His wife made him President,' thought John T. Stuart. 'She had the fire, will, and ambition.'[37]

The Lincolns had four sons together. One, Eddie, died as a toddler, and another, Willie, passed away in 1862 at the age of 7. A third child, Thomas, known as Tad, died at the age of 18, in 1871, after his father's death. Only Robert, the eldest son and the one with whom Lincoln had the most distant relationship, survived into adulthood. Lincoln was a very different father to his sons – especially to Willie and Tad – than his own father had been to him. He was, recalled a neighbour, 'tender and affectionate to his children' and gave them great latitude. In the White House, the boys ran wild, driving the servants to distraction, firing on the Cabinet with a toy cannon and racing down the Executive Mansion's corridors in a makeshift carriage hauled by a raucous pet goat. By indulging his sons, perhaps Lincoln was reacting to the harshness of his own upbringing. Perhaps, too, Lincoln was vicariously savouring his boys' carefree lack of responsibilities, while in a careful, painstaking and conscientious way he began to build his own life.

4

Harbinger of War

As a nation of freemen, we must live through all time, or die by suicide.

Abraham Lincoln

By the time he was 30, Lincoln was a state legislator and a partner in a prosperous law firm in the growing state capital, Springfield. With his dusty stove-pipe hat, his ill-fitting linen coat, trousers that never quite reached his boots and a tatty cotton umbrella tied together with a piece of coarse string to keep it from flapping, he was a distinctive figure. In 1838 he gave a speech to the city's Young Men's Lyceum. His theme was that the only danger to the American republic came from within. 'If destruction be our lot,' he prophesised, 'we must ourselves be its author and finisher. As a nation of freemen, we must live through all time, or die by suicide.'[38] He told his audience that they should respect the laws – laws that they, as free enfranchised men, had a hand in making – and he warned that mob rule was the greatest threat to republican liberty. It is likely that he had in mind as he spoke a nasty incident in the town of Quincy, Illinois, on the banks of the Ohio River only two months before, when a pro-slavery mob had murdered Elijah P. Lovejoy, the editor of an abolitionist newspaper.

At the time of the American Revolution, slavery was legal everywhere in the thirteen colonies: enslaved Africans worked as domestic servants in the townhouses of New York as well as Charleston. But in the aftermath of the Revolution, slavery was abolished in the northernmost states, where black people were relatively few in number and inconsequential to the local economy. In Virginia, Thomas Jefferson – author of the Declaration of Independence which proclaimed that 'all men are created equal' – agonised about the problem of slavery while owning dozens of slaves himself and maintaining a long-term relationship with an enslaved woman named Sally Hemmings. In old age in the 1820s, Jefferson continued to worry on the subject. No man, he claimed, would 'sacrifice more' to remove the 'heavy reproach' of slavery, were it possible to do so. Yet how could it be done safely? 'We have the wolf by the ear, and we can neither hold him, nor safely let him go,' he fretted. 'Justice is in one scale, and self-preservation in the other.'[39]

By the time Lincoln made his Lyceum speech a decade later such slaveholder hand wringing rarely happened, even in private. The enslaved population in the southern states was rising fast, as were the prices of 'prime field hands' advertised in local newspapers and in the slave auctions held in every sizable southern town. Slavery's brutality did not diminish its dynamism, and southern planters were full participants in a thriving global trade. Slavery enabled the production of cotton, the wonder crop of the nineteenth century: the raw material for the steam-powered textile factories of the industrial heartlands in Britain and elsewhere. The US South totally dominated the world cotton market, producing, for example, more than 80 per cent of the raw material imported into the UK each year by the 1850s. So white southerners no longer agonised about slavery. If slavery was a wolf, they rode it with gusto, or pretended to.

The renewed commitment of southerners to what they euphemistically called their 'peculiar institution' was partly driven by the profit motive, and partly by a conviction that social order depended on it. Meanwhile, inspired in part by the success of their British counterparts, American abolitionists set up newspapers, held meetings, published pamphlets and began petition drives. The early to mid-1830s were the years when this activity took off. In response, southern states tightened their slave laws and shut down debate whenever they could. Even in the US Congress, southern representatives pushed through so-called 'gag rules' to prevent any debate on abolitionist petitions. Some of the worst flashpoints were battles over whether to allow new slave states into the Union. Compromises were worked out: Missouri was admitted with protection for slavery in its state constitution, but Congress passed a resolution that any future states admitted north of a line on the map drawn west across the Great Plains would be free, while those to the south would be open to slavery. The hope was that this measure would settle for all time the future of slavery on the continent, ensuring that it would remain a southern institution which northerners could, if they wished, simply ignore.

The abolitionist campaign had been long and difficult in Britain, but in America it faced even greater obstacles: slaveholders, politically dominant in their own states and able to block action at the Federal level through the endless checks and balances of the Constitution, were far more powerful adversaries than was the slave interest in the UK. A compromise built into the negotiations over the new Constitution in 1787 meant that slave states were able to include three-fifths of their slaves in the calculation of how many members of the House of Representatives and Electoral College Votes for the President each state would have. This was the ultimate example of having one's cake and eating it too: enslaved people could be bought and sold like horses and they had, in the words of Roger B. Taney, Chief Justice of the Supreme Court, 'no rights which the white man was bound to respect' – yet southerners were simultaneously able to benefit from their presence when it came to political representation in Washington. The Federal structure of American government entrenched slaveholders' power too. Whereas parliament in Westminster could – and eventually did – pass a bill abolishing slavery throughout the British Empire, Congress in Washington could do no such thing because slavery was regulated by the individual states. Only a Constitutional Amendment could give legal sanction to abolition throughout the entire country and that seemed impossible to achieve, requiring, as it did, three-quarters of the states to ratify it.

Divided as the nation was, the incentives to paper over the cracks were immense, not least because this did not seem to be a problem that could be resolved through any normal political means. The national leadership of the Whig and Democratic parties, needing to appeal to voters in the North as well as the South, had a vested interest in downplaying the problem of slavery. The power of slaveholders was so entrenched that to attack them seemed likely to drive them to disunion. Furthermore, to most northerners, abolitionists were, at best, Utopian cranks and, at worst, unhinged Jacobins. In 1837, the Illinois state legislature endorsed a resolution condemning abolitionists. But it went further than that: echoing the increasingly absolutist claims of the South, the legislature asserted that, whereas a state may ban slavery if it wished (as Illinois had done), the Federal Constitution protected slave 'property' just as much as any other kind of property. The vote in the state Senate was unanimous, and in the lower House the measure was passed by seventy-seven votes to six. This vote marked Lincoln out for his relative moderation on this question because he was one of the six dissenters, a stand for which there was no possible calculation of personal political advantage.

Lincoln was no radical; he agreed that 'the promulgation of abolition doctrines tends rather to increase than abate [slavery's] evils'. But he could not support the majority's position because, while he accepted that an individual southern state was entitled to make property rules as it thought fit, he believed that the nation as a whole could not – or should not – follow suit. Although this was merely a symbolic vote in a non-slaveholding state, little noticed outside Springfield at the time, it captured the basic problem that was later to convulse the country: was it possible for two different legal systems – one recognising human property, the other founded on individual liberty – to co-exist within the same nation? Slaveholders needed continual reassurance that the Federal government was on their side. If not, would their slave property be safe? Lincoln and his five dissenting colleagues refused to give the South the guarantees they were looking for. And they added, by way of explanation, the seemingly mild observation that slavery was 'founded on both injustice and bad policy'.[40] This formulation was cautious enough that even Thomas Jefferson, in certain moods, might once have endorsed it. Yet it marked Lincoln out as one of the most strongly antislavery elected officials in Illinois in the late 1830s. As would become clearer over the next twenty years, there was ultimately no middle ground on this question: either one conceded slaveholders' demands that their 'property rights' be recognised by the national government, as the great majority of Illinois legislators were willing to do, or, however mildly, one did not.

While this episode is evidence of Lincoln's strong dislike of slavery, like most people living in free states, he had very little direct knowledge of the reality of the lives of enslaved people. Lincoln's antislavery politics were, primarily, rooted in a principled objection to the idea that one man should live off the fruits of another's labour, rather than in a visceral response to oppression. In 1841, returning by river to Springfield after a stay with the newly married Joshua Speed in Kentucky, Lincoln encountered 'ten or a dozen' slaves shackled together on the boat, perhaps being 'sold down the river', as the contemporary phrase had it, from a Kentucky owner to a more profitable plantation in the Deep South. Fourteen years later, in a letter to Speed, Lincoln described the sight as a 'continual torment to me'.[41] But at the time, in a letter to Speed's half sister, he was less emphatic. While musing on the slaves' separation from their families and their harsh conditions on the boat ('strung together precisely like so many fish upon a trot-line'), he nevertheless thought them, paradoxically, 'the most cheerful and apparently happy creatures on board' – seemingly more fascinated by their acceptance of their fate than their degradation.[42]

In the late 1840s, Lincoln served two years in the US Congress as a representative from the Illinois district that included Springfield. His term was dominated by the war that broke out between the United States and Mexico resulting in the occupation and annexation by the US of a vast area of Mexican territory, including California. Lincoln criticised the war as an unprovoked act of aggressive expansion. Like some other Whigs and an important faction of northern Democrats, he objected to the Democratic administration's militaristic foreign policy on principle and also worried, on a more pragmatic level, that admitting vast new territory annexed from Mexico would reignite the slavery controversy. In this, Lincoln was prescient. Yet neither his antislavery nor his anti-war stances prevented him from campaigning enthusiastically in 1848 for the Whig presidential candidate, Louisiana slaveholder Zachary Taylor, a Mexican War hero. In a rare national victory for any Whig, Taylor won – but Lincoln's own political career stalled. He did not seek re-election to Congress, maintaining an agreement with fellow Springfield Whigs to 'rotate' the office. Such was the Democrats' domination of state politics that apart from the one Whig-leaning congressional district that Lincoln had represented, there were few other routes to office open to him. In his early forties, his political career seemed to have foundered. 'With me,' he lamented, 'the race of ambition has been a failure – a flat failure.'[43] He returned to the law full time.

In about 1850, one of Lincoln's legal colleagues predicted that 'the time would soon come … when we must be Democrats or Abolitionists'. A middle path would no longer be possible. 'When that time comes,' replied Lincoln, 'my mind is made up.'[44] That time for choosing came in 1854. In that year, Lincoln started making political speeches again, outraged, as so many other northerners were, by the Kansas-Nebraska Act. On the surface, this was a straightforward measure to do something that all agreed was necessary: set up territorial governments for a huge area of largely unsettled land to the west of Illinois, not least so that a transcontinental railroad could be built connecting California with the East. But in order to secure support from southern congressmen for the measure, the bill's sponsor, an old sparring partner of Lincoln's, Democratic Illinois Senator Stephen A. Douglas, agreed to include a clause allowing at least the possibility that slavery might be legal in the new territories. This required the repeal of the 1821 formula, agreed at the time of the admission of Missouri, which had stated that slavery would be banned from any future territories and subsequently states established at that latitude. Douglas, a short man whose girth steadily expanded with both his own political success and the breadth of his ambition for western settlement, was convinced that this concession to the slave interest was a price worth paying for the goal of white settlement from ocean to ocean. And although he knew it would cause a storm of protest (he claimed he could travel home to Chicago from Washington by the light of his own burning effigy), he thought he had found a winning formula which, when people understood it properly, would resolve the conflict over slavery forever: let the people decide, at the local level, whether they wanted it or not. *Popular sovereignty* – and what could be more in tune with the American tradition than that? – would be applied. If the people of Kansas wanted slavery, they could have it. If they didn't, they could ban it.

To Lincoln, the Kansas-Nebraska Act was a dark betrayal, and he was not alone. The strength of the northern reaction revealed the limits to their acceptance of slavery. The Whig party, riven by internal disputes over other issues and fatally divided on sectional lines, could not provide an effective umbrella for all those who opposed the Kansas-Nebraska Act. Northern Democrats were divided too. Many followed Douglas' lead, pleading with fellow northerners to keep morality out of politics in order to maintain the Union. Others – including some influential Democratic leaders in Illinois – joined Whigs like Lincoln in believing that this latest assertion by the southern 'Slave Power' was a threat to the liberty of white northerners. The consequence was a revolution in party politics. By 1856, old Whigs and disaffected Democrats in the free states had formed the new antislavery Republican Party. The insurgent Republicans, channelling widespread popular dissatisfaction with 'politics as usual' and claiming to represent the interests of northern whites as no one else could, challenged Democratic dominance even in strongholds like Illinois. They were antislavery, but they were emphatically not abolitionists: the Republican Party did not campaign for the abolition of slavery where it already existed (something that was impossible, in any case, under the Constitution). Instead, they argued that it should be quarantined – prevented from spreading into new territory, thus preserving the West for settlement by poor white men, unimpeded by rich slave owners who might monopolise the land, and without the threat of forced labour degrading wages and opportunity for white people.

Lincoln rose to national prominence as a leader of this new party. He warned of a sinister 'Slave Power Conspiracy', an unholy alliance of southern slaveholding 'aristocrats' and northern Democratic collaborators like Stephen Douglas. Slavery, Lincoln argued, was tolerable only so long as it was an exception to the general rule of freedom, restricted geographically and understood to be – in a phrase he used again and again – 'in the course of ultimate extinction'.[45] In the face of claims from the South that Republicans were 'Jacobins' and 'revolutionaries', Lincoln presented his position as profoundly conservative: all he wanted was to return slavery to 'the position our fathers gave it; and there let it rest in peace'. 'Let us,' he declared, turn slavery back upon 'its existing legal rights, and its arguments of "necessity"'.[46] In a speech in Peoria, Illinois, in 1854, Lincoln expressed the shame and anger so many northerners felt at the expansion of slavery:

'Our republican robe is soiled and trailed in the dust,' he declared. 'Let us repurify it. Let us turn and wash it white, in the spirit, if not the blood of the Revolution.'[47] A journalist for the *Chicago Tribune* recalled that the 45-year-old lawyer's speech:

> went to the heart because it came from the heart … Mr. Lincoln's eloquence was of the higher type which produced conviction in others because of the conviction of the speaker himself. His listeners felt that he believed every word he said, and that, like Martin Luther, he would go to the stake rather than abate one jot or tittle of it.[48]

As the New England literary journal, the *Atlantic Monthly*, put it, slavery had come to seem to large numbers of northerners as rather like 'the evil fairy of the nursery tale', present at the nation's birth to 'curse it with her fatal words'.[49]

In 1858, in the run-up to the Illinois state elections, Lincoln went head to head with the author of the Kansas-Nebraska Act in seven debates. In the end, the Democrats retained their majority in the state legislature and Stephen Douglas was returned as the US Senator to Washington rather than Lincoln. But newspapers around the country reprinted the speeches of the two men verbatim and gave Lincoln the profile he needed to capture the presidential nomination of the Republican Party two years later.

In his debates with Douglas, Lincoln's main theme was the idea that Slave Power, abetted by its northern

Democratic accomplices, had corrupted the white South and was now attempting to maintain and expand its control of the national government. Ultimately, Lincoln argued, the United States would become either a slave nation or a modern free-labour nation. The time had come to be clear about the final destination. Inspiring an international liberal movement, the battle over slavery, he said, was part of:

> the eternal struggle between these two principles – right and wrong – throughout the world … The one is the common right of humanity and the other the divine right of kings … No matter in what shape it comes, whether from the mouth of a king who seeks to bestride the people of his own nation and live by the fruit of their labor, or from one race of men as an apology for enslaving another race, it is the same tyrannical principle.[50]

The issue in America was a manifestation of a great worldwide battle between those who sought to exploit others for their own profit and the alternative principle that – at least in their right to earn their own living – all men were created equal. There was, Lincoln now argued, an inherent conflict between these two claims that could no longer be ignored. His most famous – and, to some, notorious – formulation of this idea came in a speech on the steps of the Capitol building in Springfield on 16 June 1858. 'A house divided against itself cannot stand,' he warned. 'We must become all one thing or all another.'[51]

This, many listeners concluded, was the sound of a battle standard being raised. It was not the speech of a moderate conciliator but of a sectional warrior.

By connecting the issue of black slavery to the fundamental republican themes of liberty versus tyranny, Lincoln – and other Republican leaders – helped to build a northern majority for the new party, drawing support from people whose innate racism had never previously moved them to see slavery as a problem. In 1860, Abraham Lincoln captured the Republican nomination for President in a convention that took place in Chicago, in his home state. He was not the favourite, but better-known figures such as New York Senator William H. Seward or Ohio Senator Salmon P. Chase had more enemies. They were also perceived to be less effective vote-getters in the key swing states of Illinois, Indiana and Pennsylvania, where Republicans needed to expand their support. Despite his 'house divided' speech, Lincoln had a less radical record than his two main rivals and his homespun life story could be packaged to appeal to former Democrats in the Midwest. In the face of a divided Democratic Party (Stephen Douglas ran as the official Democratic candidate, but even he was now regarded as too antislavery by many southern Democrats who supported an alternative candidate instead), most political observers concluded as early as August that a Republican victory was inevitable. In November, the Electoral College system duly gave Lincoln victory even though he won only 40 per cent of the popular vote nationally and almost nobody (apart from handful of hardy abolitionists in

Missouri and Kentucky) voted for him in any slave state. His route to victory was simple enough: there were more Electoral College votes in free states than in slave states, and Lincoln won almost all of them.

Antislavery men welcomed Lincoln's election as a decisive break with the past. Since John Quincy Adams of Massachusetts left office in 1829, the national government had been continuously in the hands of either slaveholders or northern supporters of slavery. No more. Lincoln had been elected on a platform committed to ending the expansion of slavery as a 'relic of barbarism'. In Boston, Quincy Adams' son, Charles Francis Adams, was elated. 'The great revolution has actually taken place', he pronounced, and 'the country has once and for all thrown off the domination of the slaveholders'.[52] Angry southerners agreed that Lincoln's election amounted to a revolution, and some saw no alternative but to stage a counter-revolution to protect their honour and vital interests.

There were four months between Lincoln's election in November 1860 and his formal inauguration as President in March 1861. In those months seven southern states declared secession from the Union and formed a separate republic, the Confederate States of America, modelled in almost every respect on the United States but with slavery guaranteed forever. Secession was a bold and, as it turned out, reckless move, but since the Federal government was small in size and scope compared to local and state governments, in some ways the establishment of a separate Confederacy required less institutional upheaval than might be imagined. State governments continued to operate exactly as they always had – levying taxes, providing limiting services and subsidies. But the important point was the rejection of the authority of the United States as a nation. They insisted, plausibly, that as sovereign entities that had freely contracted to join the Union in the first place, seceding states did not feel they needed to invoke a right of revolution. Southerners were merely withdrawing, through due process, from a Union now run by those they felt had demeaned them. The South Carolina government was clear about the nub of the problem: the new President's party had denounced 'as sinful the institution of Slavery'. Twenty-three years after Lincoln had warned that the only route to national destruction was through 'suicide', he took office as President with the division of the nation seemingly an accomplished fact.

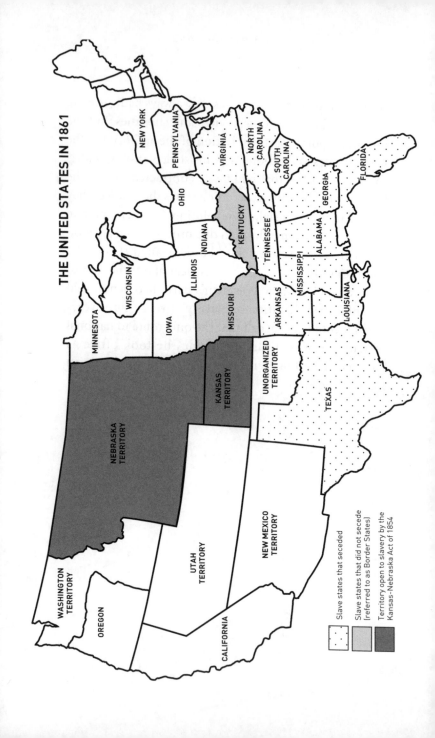

THE UNITED STATES IN 1861

Slave states that seceded

Slave states that did not secede (referred to as Border States)

Territory open to slavery by the Kansas-Nebraska Act of 1854

5

Nationalist

Plainly, the central idea of secession, is the essence of anarchy.

Abraham Lincoln

There were three ways in which northerners could have responded to secession in the winter of 1860–61. The first was to accept disunion. A few voices urged this course; after all, secession appeared to be the will of the (white) southern people and the United States was founded, as the Declaration of Independence put it, on the principle that government should be based on the 'consent of the governed'. A second option was to conciliate the South and urge peaceful reunion. Many called for this, including most Democrats, who tended to blame Republicans for stirring up the crisis over slavery at least as much as hot-headed southerners. During the secession winter Lincoln faced many calls to compromise his party's absolute opposition to the expansion of slavery into the western territories. On this, Lincoln could not have been clearer. 'Stand firm,' he told a fellow Republican. 'The tug has to come, & better now, than any time hereafter.'[53] Lincoln, in effect, chose the third option available to northerners: he refused to recognise the legitimacy of secession or make any concession to 'rebels'. At first, he told visitors that he didn't believe the threats to secede: this was no more than the latest piece of brinkmanship in the sectional tug of war.[54] Convinced of the latent unionism of most southerners – and placing much faith in his own ability to discern the true feelings of white southerners on the grounds that he himself had been born in a slave state – Lincoln underestimated the deadly seriousness of the South. The concessions he was prepared to make, such as offering a Cabinet position to a southerner, were trivial in the face of the coming storm.

For Lincoln, the nation was the fundamental unit, the ultimate embodiment of a people's political ideas and values. If it 'died' through 'suicide', the principles that gave life to the nation would perish also. 'Secession', he warned in his Inaugural Address as President, was 'the essence of anarchy'.[55] Breaking up the nation in response to a lawful election, no matter that it was dressed up in the formal language of resolutions, was the moral equivalent of mob violence. If the rebels won, Lincoln declared, it would signal an effective 'end to free government upon the earth'.[56] This iron certainty that defeating secession was essential for the survival of liberty around the world was the bedrock of Lincoln's response to the crisis. Almost every time he made a speech he found a way of formulating this idea, and from it he never wavered.

Lincoln's view of the nation was one he had imbibed from the culture in which he grew up; he may have expressed his nationalist convictions in especially eloquent ways, but his opinions were commonplace. Schoolchildren learned by rote the peroration from an 1830 speech by the Whig leader Daniel Webster ending, 'Liberty and Union, now and forever, one and inseparable!' Preachers endorsed the idea that God had specially endowed the Union with a divine purpose to spread liberty. No matter that the Union had, in reality, protected slavery for decades or that Americans did not have a worldwide monopoly on the idea of freedom, to many northerners of Lincoln's generation it seemed a self-evident truth that to break up the Union was to destroy liberty. This popular nationalism explains why a majority of northerners, led by Lincoln, were prepared to suffer and inflict a massive cost in human lives in order to preserve the political authority of the United States government. From the firing of the first shot to the final surrender, Lincoln's overriding concern was to prevent any territorial dismemberment of his country, no matter how high the price that had to be paid. When we assess Lincoln's historical role – in helping to bring about the end of slavery or as an inspiring advocate for the idea of democracy – we need to weigh into the balance the bloody consequences of his utterly unwavering faith in what he called the 'mystic chords' that bound the Union together. He never recognised the legitimacy of the Confederate government, referring to them always as rebels. For him, the war, when it came, was a vast police operation, far greater in scale, but similar in principle, to the use of force by a city's authorities to put down a riot.

The war came, as wars often do, through a combination of calculation, misunderstanding, bravado and accident. The drama centered on Fort Sumter, an island in the middle of Charleston Harbor, built to defend the city from the sea. After the government of South Carolina announced its secession it set about taking control of Federal government property in the state, but Sumter held out. The garrison there had refused to surrender to local South Carolina forces. The Stars and Stripes still flew, clearly visible to the secessionists of Charleston, as a standing rebuke to their claims to have left the United States. The question was how long the US garrison could hold out in Fort Sumter without being able to stock up on food from the mainland.

In the first weeks of his administration, Lincoln sent out mixed messages about what he planned to do about it. One of his emissaries seems to have told the governor of South Carolina that the President was so determined to avoid war that he would surrender the fort. At other times, he appeared determined to make a stand. Historians have usually given Lincoln credit for adroitly manoeuvring the Confederates into firing the first shot. While that was certainly a good outcome for Lincoln, since it allowed him to portray southerners as the aggressors, it was more the product of accident than design. Lincoln's Cabinet endorsed what they may have imagined to be a middle path: Sumter would be resupplied with food but not reinforced or re-armed. This was not a distinction that South Carolinians accepted or trusted, and when news leaked that a US naval ship was on its way to Sumter, the new Confederate government took the decision to open fire. After courteously informing the Union commander at Sumter of their intentions in advance, artillery shells were fired from the shore at the fortified island. It was not much of a battle: the only casualty was a mule. The next day the Federal garrison surrendered and was allowed safe passage back to the North. This was the theatrical, almost bloodless, opening of what was to become one of the most savage wars in modern history.

The image of southerners literally firing on the American flag stirred an extraordinary popular response in the North, with immediate demands for a massive military reprisal. Even before any official action was taken, tens of thousands of young men found weapons and makeshift uniforms, and prepared to teach the southerners a lesson. With seemingly little political alternative, Lincoln chose to go to war. He sent a message to state governors asking for troops to put down the rebellion. Appalled at being asked to join in the armed invasion of sister slave states, four states that had not yet seceded – North Carolina, Tennessee, Arkansas and Virginia – felt compelled to join the Confederacy. For those Upper South states in that heated moment, the issue was no longer a calculation of how best to protect their slave property, but a re-enactment of their forefathers' armed defence of their liberties against a tyrannical government. Richmond, Virginia, now became the capital of the Confederacy, barely 90 miles – and, in theory, just three days' march – from the Federal capital.

In 1861, millions of Americans went to war believing this was their generation's opportunity to earn a place in history on a par with their Revolutionary forebears. The problem of slavery in the United States was a lethal cocktail of economic interest, morality and nationalism. It provoked a conflict that democratic politics proved unable to resolve. In fact, popular government fanned the flames of sectionalism, since politicians in both the North and South felt compelled to respond to the indignation of voters. The public's impatience at any prospect of a compromise deal forged in a cigar-fogged congressional chamber brought the fighting closer. The war, Lincoln said in July 1861, was a 'people's contest', by which he meant it would determine the survival of democracy. But the phrase resonates in a different sense because this was a war the people wanted, naive as they were about the slaughter to come.

6

War Leader

Doesn't it seem strange that I should be here – I, a man who couldn't cut a chicken's head off – with blood running all around me?

Abraham Lincoln

A short military adventure was easy to envisage. A long war, however, would present enormous challenges. How could a nation with no tradition of compulsory military service (other than in ramshackle local militia), with a tiny standing army and a highly decentralised government, possibly wage a long war of the kind that Britain and France had fought in the Napoleonic era? How could the government raise men and money without undermining the cherished tradition of self-rule? And might frequent elections and freedom of speech co-exist with the wartime pressure for unity? Before long it became clear that these were the questions northerners would have to grapple with. The first wave of troops signed up for just three months, and one sweeping Napoleonic victory was expected to bring final resolution. No such victory came. Instead, the first major confrontation of the war in July 1861, near a creek called Bull Run just outside Washington DC, ended with Union troops in disorganised retreat, with fleeing reporters and spectators, including some congressmen and their wives who had followed the army with picnic hampers to watch the spectacle.

In the four years of war that followed, few aspects of American life were left untouched. The war led to a vast expansion in the power of the Federal government. Huge loans were raised from private lenders and a national paper currency – the notes known as 'greenbacks' – was introduced for the first time. Lincoln assumed ever-greater executive powers to prosecute the war, consulting Congress as little as possible, and on several occasions openly defied direct rulings from the Supreme Court. In his first few weeks in office he ordered the arrest and imprisonment without trial of Confederate sympathisers in Maryland and, in 1862, he suspended the writ of *habeas corpus* nationwide for cases of 'disloyalty'. He backed up the military commander who used this suspension to arrest a prominent Ohio Democrat, Clement L. Vallandigham, who opposed the war. 'He was arrested', Lincoln insisted, because by 'encouraging desertions' he was 'damaging the army … upon which the life of the nation depends'. To those who protested that Lincoln was violating the Constitution and the traditional liberties on which it rested, he responded, unapologetically, that this was unavoidable: 'Are all the laws, *but one*, to go unexecuted, and the government itself go to pieces, lest that one be violated?'[57] This was a compelling argument to those who shared Lincoln's unshakeable belief that the political authority of the national government must be, and could only be, sustained through force. To others, including millions of northern Democrats, Lincoln's willingness to ignore or defy legal and Constitutional procedure was a terrifying betrayal of the principles for which the Union was supposed to stand.

At the centre of it all, conscious of a divine providence that had placed on him an awesome responsibility, was

Lincoln, waking before dawn and working late into the night, scribbling memos, making patronage appointments and spending long hours in the telegraph office of the nearby War Department, waiting anxiously for dispatches from the seat of battle. When he arrived in Washington, he was painfully conscious of his lack of administrative experience and military knowledge. His few weeks of 'fighting mosquitoes', as he put it, in the Black Hawk War thirty years earlier were scant preparation for the task ahead.[58] Nevertheless, he has often been credited with grasping the strategic imperatives of the conflict quicker than most of his generals. Whereas he delegated foreign affairs in large part to his Secretary of State, the urbane William H. Seward, and economic policy to Congress, he regarded the conduct of the war as primarily his own responsibility and he applied himself to it with the rigour, concentration and logical intensity that he had brought to previous challenges in his life.

As commander-in-chief, Lincoln quickly appreciated that the North's main advantage was its superiority in manpower and material resources. Knowing that the South had fewer men and only a tiny manufacturing base from which to supply arms, Lincoln recognised the need to apply consistent pressure on the Confederates in as many points as possible, simultaneously.

In the West, the strategy was fairly simple: gain control of the Mississippi valley and choke off the Confederacy's supplies. In this, despite massive loss of life at Shiloh, Stones River, Chickamauga and other places, there was steady success. New Orleans fell to Union forces in

1862 and, in July 1863, with the collapse of the heavily defended river town of Vicksburg, the Mississippi River was entirely in Union hands and the Confederate territory was cut in two. Union forces, led by General William T. Sherman, then advanced through the Appalachians and into the cotton- and slave-rich lowlands, reaching Atlanta, Georgia, by the summer of 1864.

In the East, where most of the warfare was concentrated in northern Virginia in the land between Washington DC and the Confederate capital in Richmond, the Union army ran into the formidable charisma and tactical brilliance of General Robert E. Lee. A career army officer with a genteel determination, Lee took command of Confederate forces in Virginia in May 1862 and immediately went on the offensive, shocking the Union commander, the painstaking, cripplingly cautious General George B. McClellan, with a series of brilliant victories. Lee's army proved repeatedly that they were swifter and more imaginative, inflicting defeats on numerically larger forces.

Again and again the Confederate President, Jefferson Davis, repeated that his new republic simply wanted to be left alone; however, for three reasons, southerners had little choice except to go on the offensive. First, southern public opinion demanded and expected military glory. Second, the Confederate generals believed, based on the experience of brilliant Napoleonic victories, that military advantage lay with the attacking side in any conflict. Third, the imperative to defend slavery required that 'abolitionist' Yankee invaders be challenged wherever they appeared on southern soil. Through most of the first three years of the war, the Confederate armies were victorious in enough of the biggest battles – often in spectacular style – to convince southerners that the war could ultimately be won, despite the slow and steady Union advances into the Mississippi valley. Union generals who wanted to pursue a limited war, perhaps in the belief that southern civilians could be won over, were confronted by the reality of determined and systematic military aggression by the Confederates.

The Civil War has often been called the 'first modern war'. It was a media war. Reporters followed armies everywhere, telegraphing their dispatches, and special editions of newspapers gave hourly updates to readers thousands of miles behind the lines when a great battle was in progress. At the same time, technological change since the Napoleonic conflict shifted the tactical advantage to defending forces and contributed to the horrific casualty rates. Rifled muskets, which were far more accurate and had a longer range than their predecessors, made it possible for defenders to repulse an attacking force from several hundred yards away. Sharpshooters, picking off enemies from behind cover, became increasingly effective. In December 1862, at Fredericksburg, a heavily defended town on the Rappahannock River in Virginia, the Army of the Potomac suffered more than 12,000 casualties in a futile effort to cross the river and take the town against well-entrenched defenders, earning the Union commander, General Ambrose E. Burnside, the nickname 'the butcher of Fredericksburg'. Petersburg, in 1864, scarred with barbed wire, craters made by artillery bombardments and lines of entrenchments, resembled the Somme fifty-two years later.

Yet the public, the press and even most military commanders still saw war in terms of knightly heroism and gallant assaults – preferably bayonet charges. The very notion of being able to kill a man without seeing him seemed abhorrent. Lincoln was quicker than most to understand the macabre arithmetic of this kind of warfare. Although, at Fredericksburg, Union forces lost twice as many men as the rebels, the disparity in the size of the forces meant that 'if the same battle were to be fought over again, every day, though a week of days, with the same relative results, the army under Lee would be wiped out to its last man … [and] the war would be over'.[59]

Too often in the first three years of the war, Union generals did not exploit the occasional victories they won. In September 1862, Confederate forces under Lee's command marched into Maryland, one of four slave states that had not seceded. They were forced back into Virginia after a vicious confrontation at Antietam in which 3,650 men were killed and more than 17,000 wounded. But to Lincoln's immense frustration, McClellan, having won a limited victory, refused to pursue the retreating Confederate troops, arguing that his horses and men needed to rest. Less than a year later, McClellan having been dismissed, a new Union commander, General George G. Meade, inflicted on Lee his first clear-cut defeat at Gettysburg – but Meade also allowed Lee's army to retreat back over the Potomac River into Virginia. Lincoln was especially irritated by an order Meade had issued to his men calling on them to 'drive from our soil every vestige of the presence of the invader'. The implication that the job was done so long as Confederate forces were back in Virginia seemed to sum up what Lincoln thought was the limpness of the Union military campaign in the East. 'Will our generals never get that idea out of their heads?' Lincoln fumed. 'The *whole country* is our soil.'[60]

Only in 1864, when General Ulysses S. Grant was put in charge of all Union forces, did Lincoln finally have a commander committed to attacking the Confederates day after day and on all possible fronts. Grant was a stocky, hard-drinking westerner who had struggled with business failure and alcoholism before the war, but had come into his own in the western theatre as a pugnacious commander. While the overall strategy of Union forces was to deprive the South of the will and capacity to continue fighting, in Virginia, as Lincoln realised, the only target that mattered was Lee's army. 'Wherever the enemy goes, let our troops go also,' Grant telegraphed Lincoln in August 1864. 'This,' replied Lincoln, 'is exactly right.'[61] Grant, Lincoln once observed, was 'the quietest little man you ever knew' but, unlike previous commanders, he took responsibility and 'wherever he is, things move!'[62]

By the spring of 1864, two Union soldiers were dying for every Confederate soldier killed – at the Wilderness, Cold Harbor, Spotsylvania and Petersburg. But the North, with more manpower, could stand the losses better than the increasingly beleaguered South. After the capture of Atlanta in September 1864, General William T. Sherman led his troops on his notorious march to the Atlantic coast, wreaking destruction in his wake. 'Southerners', warned one Union general, were to be 'swept away by the hand of God, like the Jews of old'. In London, the magazine *Punch* published an illustration that grimly depicted Lincoln and Grant's strategy as 'The American Juggernaut', a heavy artillery gun pushed by hellish banshees crushing Lilliputian figures beneath its wheels.

Many northerners saw only divine justice at work, but Lincoln and Grant's means to victory shocked even some of their supporters. 'Our bleeding, bankrupt, almost dying country ... shudders at the prospect of fresh conscriptions ... and of new rivers of human blood,' warned the *New York Tribune* in July 1864.[63] The death toll was so immense that it was barely comprehensible. 'Doesn't it seem strange,' Lincoln once remarked to a congressman, 'that I should be here – I, a man who couldn't cut a chicken's head off – with blood running all around me?'[64] Like a man who had woken to find himself still living in a nightmare, with horrific events around him seemingly beyond his control, Lincoln saw no alternative but to 'finish the work we are in'.[65] As a military leader, he had the virtues of simplicity: a clear conception of the urgency of the task and, for all his human sensitivity, a seemingly unwavering resolve that the cause was so righteous as to be worth any price.

7

Emancipator

In giving freedom to the slave, we assure freedom to the free.

Abraham Lincoln

In the Lincoln Memorial in Washington DC – a neo-classical temple that has played host to countless national events – there is no direct mention of emancipation. Instead, the monument, which houses the vast, impassive, seated statue of Lincoln, is dedicated to the memory of the man who 'saved the Union'. It was not built until the 1920s, more than half a century after Lincoln's death. Had the funds been available in the late 1860s, a very different kind of Lincoln memorial might have appeared within sight of the US Capitol. The proposed plan of that time resembled a vast marble wedding cake, with each ornate Victorian layer commemorating, in turn, soldiers who fought for the Union, the politicians who led the Union to victory, equestrian statues of the leading generals, a bas relief of the story of bondage, toil and eventual freedom of enslaved people, and finally, at the very pinnacle, a statue of Lincoln seated at a desk signing the Emancipation Proclamation. The message of the 1860s was that the pre-eminent reason to memorialise the martyred President was his role as the 'Great Emancipator'. Had that immense monument been built, not only would the public space of Washington DC look very different today, but the public image of Lincoln would have been, in all probability, vastly different as well. The actual Lincoln Memorial of the 1920s enables the visitor to focus on the nation, on military victory and on reunion, and to gloss over the issue of slavery. The one that was never built put slavery at its very heart.

The contrast between these two Lincoln memorials – the proposed and the actual – is partly a product of their political contexts. In the immediate aftermath of the war, the victorious Republicans who dominated Congress were strong supporters of emancipation and many advocated equal civil rights for black people. In the late 1860s and early 1870s, thanks to a series of Constitutional Amendments and the commitment of the Federal government to enforce equal citizenship rights, there were thousands of African American office holders in the United States, including some who had been held as property only a few years earlier. For a while there was even a black governor of South Carolina. It was the most incredible revolution in political status. But it was also fleeting. By the late 1870s, a mixture of violence, intimidation and the withdrawal of the support of the Federal government had driven most black people out of politics in the South. The long period of disenfranchisement and legally sanctioned discrimination known as Jim Crow had begun. By the 1920s, when the money was finally raised for a memorial in Washington, the Ku Klux Klan was able to march down Pennsylvania Avenue from the Capitol building to the White House and the President (a Republican, Calvin Coolidge) said nothing to discourage them. The last thing a Lincoln memorial would do in such circumstances was resuscitate the issue of black civil rights. The Civil War was to be officially commemorated in those first decades of the twentieth century as a tragic struggle among honest and noble white men. The memory of the battle for black freedom was kept alive only by small numbers of white civil rights activists, by black intellectuals like W.E.B. DuBois and in the folk memory of the black community.

These two Lincoln memorials are also metaphors for the twin poles of Lincoln interpretation offered by historians. There are those who see Lincoln as a radical figure, intent from the outset on destroying slavery as soon as he got the chance. Then there are those who see him as essentially conservative, interested only in the preservation of the Union, moving against slavery only when he felt he had no other choice. The argument that Lincoln was a tardy and reluctant emancipator rests on three claims, which are, in themselves, broadly true: that before the war Lincoln was no abolitionist; that for more than a year after war broke out he resisted calls for emancipation; and that even after the Emancipation Proclamation his commitment to black rights was uncertain. The argument that Lincoln was fundamentally committed to black freedom also rests on claims that are, insofar as they go, demonstrably right: that he had always thought slavery wrong; that he issued the Emancipation Proclamation in spite of strong advice not to do so; and that afterwards he never wavered in his commitment to end slavery, even pushing for the Thirteenth Amendment to the Constitution before the war ended in order to ensure that the issue was settled for all time.

The truth may lie not so much in the middle – if middle, in this context, means that Lincoln was simply moderate or uncertain – but in recognising that emancipation and Union were not alternatives to be played off against one another; they were inextricably fused by war. Much as he had always disapproved of slavery, it was only when emancipation became, in Lincoln's view, a tool to save the Union that he was emboldened to embrace it. Frederick Douglass, the charismatic African American abolitionist who had been born a slave, recognised this very well. Black people, Douglass said, were 'at best only [Lincoln's] stepchildren'. 'He was willing, while the South was loyal, that it should have its pound of flesh', yet in his 'heart he loathed slavery' and when the slaveholders made their war, he 'did not hesitate'. It was this 'love for union and liberty' that made Lincoln, in Douglass' words, 'doubly dear to us'.[66]

Like most other northerners, Lincoln believed in every man's right to the fruits of his own labour. Unlike some, he could not happily acknowledge a racial limit to this right. 'If A. can prove, however, conclusively that he may, of right, enslave B.,' he wrote, 'why may not B. snatch the same argument, and prove equally, that he may enslave A?' Racial inequality was no answer:

You say A. is white and B. is black. It is color then; the lighter having the right to enslave the darker? Take care. By this rule you are to be slave to the first man you meet with a fairer skin than your own. You do not mean color exactly? – You mean the whites are intellectually the superiors of the blacks, and therefore have the right to enslave them? Take care again. By this rule, you are to be a slave to the first man you meet, with an intellect superior to your own.[67]

Slavery, in other words, could never be accommodated into an idea of freedom, not even – as his adversary Stephen Douglas in practice sought to do – by suggesting that the enslavement of black people posed no threat to the freedom of whites.

Lincoln's refusal to accept racial differences as a justification for slavery did not mean he was without racial prejudice. In his 1858 debates with Stephen Douglas, he was at pains to say that he did not favour racial equality: 'I do not understand that because I do not want a negro woman for a slave I must necessarily want her for a wife.'[68] And in an 1862 meeting in the White House with a delegation of African Americans, Lincoln bluntly told them that their presence in America had been bad for both white and black people, and that it was better for the two races to be separated, with black people being colonised outside the borders of the US. There is no reason to doubt Lincoln's sincerity in these widely published remarks, not least because he continued to push colonisation plans behind the scenes for the following two years. But Lincoln's racial views were complex, and, it seems, capable of evolution. By the end of the war, he had not given up on the possibility of colonisation as a solution for some freedmen, but at the same time he mused on the possibility of giving at least some black men the vote. He never came close to advocating a genuinely bi-racial America, nor did he free himself of the prejudices of his time and place, but his racial views were more progressive than many of those around him and a good deal more nuanced than many later interpreters have acknowledged.

The outbreak of war did not automatically mean the end of slavery in America; had the conflict been resolved in a few weeks slavery would, presumably, have remained intact. But a long war was a different matter. The attempt to break up the Union and form a separate nation was driven by slaveholders. That was not just the rhetoric of the Republican Party; it was the reality. It was not so much of a step to the realisation that if, to use the language of the time, slavery was the 'tap-root' of the rebellion, the only way to be sure of stamping out the 'poison' of treason from the American body politic was to eradicate slavery. The *New York Tribune*'s standing headline above its front-page section of war reports was 'The Slave Power Rebellion'. If the Slave Power had caused the rebellion then surely slavery had to go.

In the first year of the war, Lincoln did not appear keen to act upon this insight, much to the frustration of radicals in his own party. But there were serious constraints on his ability to do so, not least the fact that four slave states – Missouri, Kentucky, Maryland and Delaware – remained in the Union, however tenuously. Maryland and Kentucky, in particular, were of immense strategic importance, the former because without it Washington DC would be an island surrounded by seceded states and the latter because of its key river systems, agricultural production and population. Maryland was kept in the Union by force (pro-secession legislators were simply locked up), but

Kentucky's loyalty in the summer of 1861 rested on delicate diplomacy: above all the promise that the war was for the restoration of the Union and not the 'revolutionary' social upheaval of emancipation. When two radical antislavery Union generals declared the freedom of enslaved people in their respective military districts, Lincoln, to the horror of abolitionists, stepped in and overruled them.

It was a delicate and paradoxical situation. Slavery was protected by the very Constitution against which slaveholders were rebelling. The central political issue of the war became how far the end (Union) justified the means. For many northerners, if the price of military victory meant opening up the Pandora's box of emancipation, it was not worth paying. This was certainly the view of the leading Union general in 1861 and 1862, George McClellan, who told Lincoln that 'forcible abolition of slavery' should not 'be contemplated for a moment'. Americans North and South still lived, in a sense, in the shadow of the slave rebellion in Haiti in the 1790s, led by Toussaint Louverture, in which thousands of white colonists had been slaughtered. Lincoln may have called secession the essence of anarchy, but to many of his fellow northerners, the real anarchic threat was the prospect of black freedom. Anti-emancipation campaigners sought to mobilise popular feeling against emancipation using lurid images of guillotines and rampaging mobs, together with the more prosaic threat of hordes of freed black people moving north in search of jobs. In the face of this, Lincoln kept reiterating that his sole purpose was to save the Union. Emancipation, he emphasised to a visiting delegation of ministers from Chicago in August 1862, was 'a practical war measure, to be decided upon according to the advantages or disadvantages it may offer to the suppression of the rebellion'.[69]

By the time Lincoln wrote these words, however, he had already decided to issue a Proclamation of Emancipation. He was waiting for a Union military victory, which eventually came (after a fashion) at Antietam in September, fearing that to declare an emancipation policy after battlefield defeats would look like an act of sheer desperation. On 22 September 1862, the President issued a proclamation stating that if, by 1 January 1863, the rebel states had not returned to the Union, the United States would regard slaves held in rebel areas as free. It was not that Lincoln seriously expected the rebel states to return to the Union in those three months, but he hoped that by giving them fair warning it would be easier to make the case that this was a war measure rather than something inspired by abolitionist zeal. Like a riot policeman warning that if the mob didn't disperse he would fire, Lincoln was consciously attempting to hold the moral and political high ground.

On 1 January, the President duly issued the Emancipation Proclamation. As the preliminary proclamation had promised, it applied only to those areas of the United States still in arms against the government. Much of the document was taken up with a list of counties in rebel states that, because they were now occupied by the Union army, were exempted from the proclamation. Then came the central point:

I do order and declare that all persons held as slaves within [rebel-controlled areas], are, and henceforward shall be free; and that the Executive government of the United States, including the military and naval authorities thereof, will recognize and maintain the freedom of said persons.[70]

As many have pointed out, both at the time and since, the Emancipation Proclamation thus declared free only those slaves the Federal government did not have the power to free while leaving alone those under Union control. In fact this was not quite true: around 20,000 slaves, mostly in Union-occupied North Carolina, were freed immediately. But in any case, this criticism of the proclamation misses the point. What Lincoln was doing was formalising a change in the aim of the war. From 1 January 1863 onwards the administration was formally committed to the controversial object of reunion *through* emancipation. The one would not be, and could not be, achieved without the other. It is ultimately futile to try to parse the issue of whether Lincoln was more committed to emancipation or to Union. For him they had become – as a result of the Slaveholder Rebellion and the difficulty of putting it down – inseparable. The Emancipation Proclamation was also a response to the reality on the ground: whatever the administration's official position, in practice enslaved people saw the Union army as a force of liberation, and had done since the war began. As early as the spring of 1861, Union outposts in Confederate states, such as at Fort Monroe in Virginia, were housing thousands of runaway slaves.

The proclamation did not, in itself, settle the future of slavery – only military victory and ultimately the Thirteenth Amendment could do that. Nor did it signal Lincoln's belief that only a forcible emancipation alone could end slavery in America. He fully recognised that it was but one part of a larger process. Again and again, he urged slaveholders in the Border States (whose 'property' was not affected by the proclamation) to accept emancipation in return for financial compensation from the Federal government (the model adopted in the British Empire). 'If the war continue long, as it must,' he warned one Border State delegation in July 1862, slavery 'in your states will be extinguished by mere friction and abrasion'. If they did not co-operate with a compensated emancipation plan, slavery would go anyway, 'and you will have nothing valuable in lieu of it'.[71] That, in the end, was exactly what happened: in stark contrast to slave owners in Brazil or the British Empire, or, for that matter, the Russian nobility who ensured that they salvaged as much as they could from the decision of Tsar Alexander II to free the serfs in 1861, American slaveholders literally went down fighting. The future status of slaves, therefore, depended on the fortunes of war. When the Confederate army was in the ascendant – for example, during Braxton Bragg's invasion of Kentucky in 1862 – the tide of emancipation was not merely stopped but reversed, as thousands of black people were re-enslaved.

President Lincoln's proclamation irrevocably altered the terms on which the war would in future be discussed and conducted, and it dramatically shifted the context in which slaves took decisions to run away. It was a bold recognition that this was no longer a war to restore the old Union, but to create something new. Above all, the proclamation enabled the enlistment of freed slaves into the Union army – not on equal terms to white people (lesser pay at first and in segregated units officered by whites) – but nevertheless 200,000 armed men were added to the Union force and deprived the other side. The sight of former slaves in arms against their former masters was both terrifying and enraging to southern whites and inspiring to slaves who remained in bondage. It was also the most tangible evidence that the power structures on which the Old South had depended were being turned upside down.

Lincoln was, therefore, committed to emancipation in the context of the destruction of the rebellion. He sought to rid the Union once and for all of the 'evil fairy's' primal curse on the American republic. Had there been no war, or had the Confederacy collapsed quickly, Lincoln could not have acted as he did against slavery. The fact that the war was so bloody and so all consuming seemed to Lincoln not simply a reason to *justify* but also to *necessitate* emancipation.

8

Poet

The dogmas of the quiet past are inadequate to the stormy present.

Abraham Lincoln

Four months after the terrible three-day battle at Gettysburg, a cemetery for the Union dead was opened just outside the town and President Lincoln travelled there by train to make a speech unveiling it. His words were elegantly arranged and few in number. His Gettysburg Address was reprinted in the newspapers the next day and, while there was some praise from sympathetic editorial writers, no one at the time thought it was especially remarkable. That was probably because Lincoln had been saying similar things for some time. And also because, as with most of his speeches, he was articulating what many ordinary northerners were saying day to day. There were no new thoughts in the Gettysburg Address. Nor did Lincoln's writing – sparse and simple, lacking artifice or learned allusion – match up to prevailing standards of eloquence. However, Lincoln was a poet in the sense that he could condense in vivid and memorable language, ideas and feelings that people knew and could relate to. In private meetings, he often did this by telling a homespun story without any affectation. A patrician New York lawyer, George Templeton Strong, recorded the following tale the President told a group of rather startled dignitaries in October 1861, in response to a question about radicals pressing the administration to adopt an emancipation policy:

'Wa-al', says Abe Lincoln, 'that reminds me of a party of Methodist parsons that was travelling in Illinois when I was a boy thar, and had a branch to cross that was pretty bad – ugly to cross, ye know, because of the waters was up. And they got considerin' and discussin' how they should git across it, and they talked about it for two hours, and one on 'ed thought they had ought to cross one way when they got there, and another way, and they got quarrellin' about it, till at last an old brother put in, and he says, says he, 'Brethren, this here talk ain't no use. I never cross a river until I come to it.'[72]

Whenever he spoke in public, in contrast, Lincoln never extemporised at all but carefully wrote out his words, even if he planned to say very little. On that November day in Gettysburg, speaking in his high-pitched Kentucky accent, the President began like this:

Four score and seven years ago, our fathers brought forth on this continent a new nation, conceived in liberty and dedicated to the proposition that all men are created equal.

This was a way of reiterating, with a solemnity that gave it the truth of chiselled granite, the idea that it was the Declaration of Independence (1776), with its soaring rhetoric about equality, that was the founding moment of the republic. It was the Declaration that was the crucial starting point for the nation and thus for Lincoln; it gave substance to the claim that the United States was unique in being, in his words, 'dedicated' to a universal ideal. The Declaration of Independence was not formally a part of the Constitution, but for Lincoln it was, as he put it on another occasion, the 'apple of gold' around which the 'picture of silver' of the Union and the Constitution had been framed, and 'the picture was made for the apple – not the apple for the picture'.[73]

At Gettysburg, echoing in secular language the Christian idea of a trial of faith, Lincoln went on to claim that the Civil War was a test of 'whether that nation or any nation so conceived and so dedicated can long endure'. The struggle and the sacrifice had a dignity and a purpose of universal and transcendent significance:

It is for us the living rather to be dedicated here to the unfinished work which they who fought here have thus far so nobly advanced. It is rather for us to be here dedicated to the great task remaining before us – that from these honored dead we take increased devotion to that cause for which they gave the last full measure of devotion – that we here highly resolve that these dead shall not have died in vain, that this nation under God shall have a new birth of freedom, and that government of the people, by the people, for the people shall not perish from the earth.[74]

Lincoln's generalisations avoided knotty problems like the future status of black people. He did not mention emancipation directly. When he talked about 'a new birth of freedom' he meant for the nation as a whole, not just for enslaved African Americans; most of his white listeners would not have taken him to be making a rallying cry to protect black rights. But less than a year after the Emancipation Proclamation, with black troops now fighting and dying for the Union, it was clear that it was the purging of slavery from the nation that would enable America to be reborn in freedom, shorn of its original sin. Nor did he mention the Confederate enemy directly. This, after all, was a war that Lincoln always understood as being fundamentally an internal one – can we govern ourselves? Can we live up to our own highest ideals, to the 'better angels of our nature'?[75]

If we want to understand why Lincoln mattered – not just in America but beyond its borders too – the Gettysburg Address is a vital part of the story. In this brief speech he offered a vision of America as a saviour of mankind, a carrier of ideas about human liberty and equality that were constantly under threat and had constantly to be striven for. And, in that long final sentence, he offered up a definition of democracy (government of, by and for the people) that was not novel (he and others had used versions of it before) but which became – in some cases literally – a banner headline demand for popular government. His words have echoed through American and global rhetoric ever since. It has been recorded by seemingly every famous American since the invention of recording devices, from Neil Armstrong to Johnny Cash. But its universality ensured that it travelled to other continents, too. It was a favourite trope of Fidel

Castro and Eamon de Valera, and also of Ulster Unionists. It was translated into French to become Article 2 of the Constitution of the Fifth Republic. The whole speech, almost exactly the same length as Hamlet's 'To be or not to be' soliloquy, is, like most great speeches, an extended metaphor, and this metaphor is the most elementary of all – birth, death and resurrection: fathers *brought forth*; these honoured *dead*; a *new birth* of freedom. From this metaphor, Lincoln dramatises the most elementary human choice: to be or not to be free? Couched in such terms, how could the Union cause not triumph?

9

Politician

With public sentiment, nothing can fail; without it, nothing can succeed.

Abraham Lincoln

As Lincoln recognised, the outcome of the American Civil War was ultimately determined by public opinion. The Union's superior manpower and resources meant that the longer the war continued, the more likely it would be to prevail so long as the northern public was prepared to bear the extraordinary cost. Conversely, the Confederacy could win only by persuading the North to stop fighting. General Lee knew this, too, which is partly why he led his army into Maryland and, later, into Pennsylvania, in the hope of bringing the destruction of war home to the North. For northerners, balancing the cost against the cause was rarely an easy calculation. Even some otherwise fervent supporters of the Union quailed at the slaughter at times, desperately clutching at the hope of alternative solutions. Lincoln, though, never wavered in his commitment to maintain the Union through whatever force was necessary, and he devoted all of his considerable political skills to keeping together a majority of northerners behind his vision of how to bring about victory.

'With public sentiment, nothing can fail; without it, nothing can succeed,' Lincoln pronounced in one of his 1858 debates with Douglas. 'Consequently,' he continued, 'he who moulds public sentiment goes deeper than he who enacts statutes and decisions possible or impossible to be executed.'[76] This insight went to the heart of Lincoln's understanding of the nature of political leadership. Secessionists, as he saw it, were engaged in 'insidious debauching of the public mind', persuading otherwise loyal citizens to rebel.[77] The same threat was present within the North. His task was to counter this influence – to bring thirty years of experience as a prairie lawyer and stump speaker to bear in educating the public mind of the utter importance of supporting the war effort. To this end, Lincoln took great care to get his words circulated in the press. A crowd of only a couple of thousand people heard Lincoln deliver the Gettysburg Address in person, but millions read it in their daily newspapers. Mid-nineteenth-century America was the world's greatest newspaper-reading society. Lincoln wrote carefully worded public letters and made numerous short speeches to delegations of soldiers who 'serenaded' him outside the White House, relying on sympathetic editors to report his words. He used the churches to disseminate his views as well, making sure that meetings he held with clergymen in the White House were reprinted in the highly influential denominational press. Twice a week, Lincoln would hold what he called his 'public-opinion baths', meeting visitors to the White House, many of them ordinary members of the public calling with favours to ask. 'Though the tax on my time is heavy,' Lincoln once said, 'no hours of my day are better employed than those which … bring me again within the direct contact and atmosphere of our whole people.'[78]

Knowing what the public felt and thought was one thing, but moving public opinion your way was not just a matter of laying out elegant arguments in reprinted speeches – though that helped. It was, fundamentally, a matter of winning elections. No one ever suggested suspending elections for the duration of the war; after all, northerners believed them to be the practical manifestation of popular government for which the war was being fought. But elections, which mixed carnival, evangelical revival meetings, gang violence and melodramatic on-stage posturing, brought conflict to the surface. While Lincoln had a majority of the vote in the free states in 1860, outside of New England his majorities were not large and a successful war could not be waged without reaching out to those who mistrusted Republicanism. One way of reaching out was to try to present the Republican Party as a much broader coalition in wartime than it had been before, not least by changing its name: Lincoln's supporters often ran under the banner of the Union Party. The more sinister consequence of this strategy was to brand electoral opposition from the Democrats as not just politically objectionable but potentially treasonous. Arguing that support for the administration was nothing less than patriotic duty, mass-membership Union leagues mobilised voters across the North – and intimidated opponents, sometimes with threats of violence.

Lincoln and his political supporters regarded Republican (or Union Party) victories in wartime elections as no less than an extension of the battle being fought against the Confederate armies. However, beneath the rhetoric of patriotic unity, Lincoln struggled even to keep together the warring factions of his own party. In

Congress, radicals assaulted him for his alleged timidity in fighting the war or embracing emancipation, while Democrats attacked him as a tyrant. Had the United States had a parliamentary rather than presidential system, Lincoln would very likely have been forced from office by a no-confidence vote. Lincoln was an even more polarising President than the dominant political figure of his youth, Andrew Jackson. To those opposed to emancipation (at least a third of the northern population, at times probably more than half), Lincoln was a Jacobinical fanatic, 'King Africanus I' who was set on 'mongrelising' the white race. He was portrayed as subverting the Constitution by suspending *habeas corpus* and defying the Supreme Court. He was considered a tyrant for introducing forcible conscription into the army.

Yet he was also loved. The sobriquet 'Father Abraham' was not a posthumous invention designed to bolster his mythological status: it was used at the time by his supporters, especially ordinary soldiers in the Union army, and it conveys something of the personal relationship that millions who had never met him felt they had with their leader. In the last ten years of his life – the period of his meteoric rise from obscurity to eminence – Lincoln had lost none of the introspection of his youth, nor his dark nights of the soul. But with success, his inner confidence grew, a marker of which was his apparent lack of any malice and his calmness in the face of intense pressure. What those who christened him 'Father Abraham' intuitively recognised was Lincoln's utter lack of pretension – a remarkable trait in someone so successful in such an ego-driven world as politics. 'If I were asked what it was that threw such charm around him,' wrote his old friend Joshua Speed, 'I would say it was his perfect naturalness. He could act no part but his own. He copied no one in either manner or style … True to nature [and] true to himself, he could be false to no one.'[79]

Political conflict within the North came to a head in the November 1864 presidential election. Lincoln's re-election was more important to the outcome of the war than any individual battle. Had he lost, the result would, rightly, have been interpreted by the Confederates as a sign that the northern will to continue the fight was fatally weakened. Democrats appealed to northerners' sense of anger and despair at the cost of the war; Lincoln appealed to their determination to finish the job. Lincoln's Democratic opponent, George B. McClellan – the former general who had opposed emancipation – insisted that he supported the military subjugation of the rebels. However, many in McClellan's party, including his running mate, did not. And, by vociferously opposing emancipation, Democrats were rejecting what Lincoln argued had become a major tool of war. If McClellan won, what would become of the freed men fighting for the Union? The Democratic platform called for an immediate cession of hostilities with the South. As Lincoln saw it, his entire political project, to save the Union and to save it, as he put it, in such a way as to make it 'forever worthy of the saving', was at stake. But at just the crucial moment – in September as the campaign was getting under way – there was a military breakthrough for the Union when Atlanta fell to General Sherman. All of a sudden the Democratic convention's declaration that the war was a failure looked embarrassingly premature. Although there would be a further six months of hard fighting, it was now difficult to doubt the Union's success, so long as it stuck to the path laid out by the administration. With this piece of good fortune, Lincoln eased to a relatively comfortable re-election, aided by strong support from soldiers, voting in their tens of thousands in makeshift polling places in army camps.

Re-election gave Lincoln the political capital he needed to complete the job, not only to back Generals Grant and Sherman in their final push against the Confederacy, but also to bring about a final, constitutionally binding resolution to the problem of slavery. Once the war was over, the Emancipation Proclamation, issued by Lincoln as commander-in-chief, would probably have carried no legal force. Only a Constitutional Amendment, duly passed by a two-thirds majority in Congress and ratified by three-quarters of the states, could ensure that slavery would be abolished forever. In January 1865, Lincoln pushed Congress to vote on exactly such an Amendment. It was rare for Lincoln to exercise political muscle over Congress. For the most part he had not needed to because his executive action had been sufficient. The previous year, Congress had failed to back the Amendment, but Lincoln now argued, with dubious plausibility given the way the issue was downplayed on the stump, that his re-election was a mandate for final emancipation. The passage of the Thirteenth Amendment through the House of Representatives on 31 January 1865 guaranteed that the end of the war would also mean an end to slavery. In the end, Lincoln's greatest political achievement was to play the leading part in building a coalition of different kinds of people in American society, all of whom, with greater or lesser enthusiasm, came to accept emancipation not just as a radical bolt-on to the war effort but as an integral part of it.

This acceptance, it should be stressed, carried no necessary ongoing commitment to black civil rights. Lincoln remained characteristically pragmatic about the future status of black people in post-war America. In his very last public speech, he warned against 'exclusive' and 'inflexible' plans that would become a 'new entanglement'. He did not approach the post-war world with a template in mind, but with a pragmatic and clear-sighted awareness of the difficulty of every possible option, of the fallibility of leaders and people, and of the necessity to keep striving in pursuit of an ideal of individual freedom and self-government.

Lincoln never had a chance to pursue a passage through the swirling waters of the post-war world, though, because at Ford's Theatre on the night of 14 April 1865, he was shot. Less than a week earlier, General Lee had surrendered to General Grant at Appomattox, a tiny village in south-west Virginia. Southern morale had finally collapsed. Lincoln had visited Richmond, now fallen to the Union army and left in smouldering ruins by the evacuating Confederates. He had sat behind the desk of the Confederate leader Jefferson Davis and, protected by a detachment of black troops, had toured the city, mobbed by black people wherever he went. 'I know I am free,' one recalled, 'for I have seen Father Abraham and felt him.'[80]

10

Martyr

Now he belongs to the ages.

Stanton, Edwin M., Hay, John & Nicolay, John
George, 'The Fourteenth of April', *Century Magazine*
39 (January 1890), p. 436

In his youth, some thought Lincoln an atheist. He was an 'avowed and open infidel' according to one who knew him.[81] His parents had been members of a Baptist sect (one that disapproved of slavery), but after the move to Indiana they had lived miles from the nearest congregation. Some of his New Salem neighbours claimed that, when he was 25, Lincoln caused a stir by penning an essay purporting to show that the Bible was not God's inspired word. Later in life – as a respectable lawyer and state politician married to a well-to-do woman in Springfield – Lincoln usually attended a Presbyterian church. He was friendly with ministers (though his humorous stories often poked fun at them) and biblical references came as naturally to him as to most other Americans. But while he spoke of God frequently, he never straightforwardly acknowledged the lordship of Jesus Christ. The evangelical Protestant revivals that swept up so many men and women of his generation appear to have left him unmoved. Having rejected the strict Calvinism of his parents, Lincoln retained a strong sense of what he sometimes called a 'doctrine of necessity' and later came to understand as God's overruling providence. This strong sense of fate intensified when the war came. The line from Exodus, 'Stand still and see the salvation of the Lord', was, he told his friend Speed at a youthful moment of crisis, 'my text just now'.[82] Later, as President, he was certain that 'I have not controlled events, events have controlled me'.[83] God's larger purposes could be discerned only through a glass darkly, but that there *were* such purposes he did not doubt. Like many of his generation, Lincoln embraced reason and the power of scientific logic while never shaking off the creeping certainty that a hidden hand was directing worldly events.

As the death toll mounted, Lincoln – an increasingly brooding and lonely figure – became more and more convinced that the Civil War was God's punishment for the sin of slavery. He conceived of the Almighty as the ruler of nations as well as of men: nations, like individuals, were moral beings with duties. While God's purposes were mysterious, he never seemed to have doubted that the American Union, under God, held out the promise of moral and political transfiguration of the world and that a purified, purged nation would emerge from the fiery trial of war. This was a common understanding among northerners by 1865. The Methodist bishop, Matthew Simpson, spoke for many when he expressed confidence that 'if the world is to be raised to its proper place, I would say it with all reverence, God cannot do without America'.[84] The nation, once redeemed, would henceforth be 'the crowning national work of the Almighty, the wonder of the world'. Yet while sharing this basic outlook, Lincoln was wary of claiming to know God's ultimate purposes. He was almost obsessed with the danger of hubris. Nations, like people, it seemed to him, were imperfectible yet should continually strive to live up to their commandments.

Lincoln's remarkable second Inaugural Address, delivered in March 1865 with the war almost won, is the ultimate expression of this sense of humility. In it, Lincoln acknowledged that the North was as culpable as the South for the sin of slavery and speculated that God gave to 'both North and South this terrible war' as retribution for their collective guilt. He continued:

> Fondly do we hope – fervently do we pray – that this mighty scourge of war may speedily pass away. Yet, if God wills that it continue, until all the wealth piled by the bond-man's two hundred and fifty years of unrequited toil shall be sunk, and until every drop of blood drawn with the lash, shall be paid by another drawn with the sword ... so still it must be said 'the judgments of the Lord, are true and righteous altogether'.[85]

'I believe it is not immediately popular,' Lincoln observed of this speech:

> Men are not flattered by being shown that there has been a difference of purpose between the Almighty and them. To deny it, however, in this case, is to deny that there is a God governing the world. It is a truth which I thought needed to be told and as whatever of humiliation there is in it, falls directly on myself, I thought others might afford for me to tell it.[86]

Lincoln's complex yet clearly articulated understanding of the nation's ethical choices has formed part of his transcendent appeal. His lack of egoism in power seemed to some, both at the time and in retrospect, to be a source of his 'greatness'. We should not doubt, however, that while he felt a larger divine purpose at work, Lincoln nevertheless consciously and strenuously sought to shape events through his own agency. In the spirit of self-making that had driven him from a rural backwater to respectability and ultimately to the national political stage, Lincoln placed his faith in purposeful action. 'We must work earnestly in the best light He gives us,' he advised, 'trusting that so working still conduces to the great ends He ordains.'[87] Lincoln's tendency to 'melancholia' may have been a spur to action: through purposeful activity, especially in a morally compelling cause, he could give meaning to his life. But ultimately what guided him was his powerful sense of the unique and universal mission of the American Union.

He died at the moment of his triumph and before the messy problems of the post-war settlement had to be confronted. Was this the final emanation of God's plan? 'Lincoln died prematurely by the hand of the assassin,' Leo Tolstoy wrote:

> but the question is, was his death not predestined by a divine wisdom, and was it not better for the nation and for his greatness that he died just in that way and at that particular moment? We know so little about that divine law which we call fate that no one can answer.[88]

Tolstoy's analysis, uttered from half a century's perspective, echoed Lincoln's own – he told those who worried about his safety that there was no use trying to stop a determined killer. The idea that Lincoln had been martyred to redeem the sins of his nation did not make his death any less shattering to the North. Newspapers reported that only the crucifixion upon Calvary had been a blacker crime in human history. 'I consider Lincoln Republicanism incarnate – with all its faults and its virtues,' wrote Lincoln's Private Secretary John Hay in 1866. 'As in spite of some rudeness, Republicanism is the sole hope of a sick world, so Lincoln with all his foibles, is the greatest character since Christ.'[89]

Lincoln's body was taken by railroad back to Springfield. The 1,000-mile route was lined with crowds gathered to pay their respects. It lay for a day in the Illinois Capitol while Lincoln's old friends and acquaintances filed past. To one of Lincoln's Springfield neighbours, his 'amazing popularity' was due to two things: 'he had been successful in the most trying circumstances and then he was most emphatically one of the People.'[90] A basically conservative man, he presided over a revolutionary transformation. A fiercely ambitious man, he did not relish or abuse the power he won. An intensely private man, he became a very public symbol, inseparable from the dramatic events that unfolded around him.

When the Italian nationalist Giuseppe Mazzini died in 1872, Italian Republicans modelled the staging of his funeral on Lincoln's, including the railway journey through the country, weeping workers and their wives presenting the Republican leader with a last salute. In 1920 the British Prime Minister David Lloyd George unveiled a statue of Lincoln opposite the Houses of Parliament in Westminster, declaring that this man, born in a log cabin on the frontier of a distant continent, was 'one of those giant figures, of whom there are very few in history, who lose their nationality in death'. And when a north-east English miners' leader dedicated his memoirs to 'Stern, Indomitable "Old Abe"', for whom 'freedom was an eternal principle; to live in the White House was a temporary fleeting', he did so mainly because he saw Lincoln as proof that an ordinary working man could ascend to the highest office, could speak in beautiful clear language and leave behind him great deeds.[91] The embodiment of democracy, the 'emancipator' of slaves and the man who ensured the survival of the United States, giving it, in the saving, a universal meaning for the 'whole family of man' – this was the Lincoln who was mourned at his death and whose image was evoked for decades to come, for many distinct and often opposing purposes, but almost always with reverence.

A Note on the Lincoln Literature

There is no space in this short biography to acknowledge in a proper manner the large scholarly literature on Abraham Lincoln on which I have drawn. The list of secondary readings below should be regarded as an indicative – perhaps rather arbitrary – guide to further reading and not a complete bibliography of works that have influenced the interpretation I have set out in these pages. However, it might be helpful to readers who wish to know more about Lincoln, but who have encountered him here for the first time, if I briefly explain in very general terms how I believe 'my' Lincoln compares to others. If, having reached the end of this book, you have the impression that I presented Lincoln in a flattering light, you may well be right. I do admire Abraham Lincoln, for his elegant prose, his remarkable capacity for humility – especially visible in his second Inaugural Address – and because, at root, he was a sincere and passionate advocate of what I believe to be a great cause: to 'elevate the condition of men [and] to lift artificial weights from all shoulders'.[92] However, you will discover if you read further into the Lincoln literature that other historians flatter him much more than I do. There are, in particular, two interrelated claims widely accepted in recent scholarship that I have consciously resisted here.

One is the argument that Lincoln underwent some sort of moral transformation from being generally indifferent to the problem of slavery (before the Kansas-Nebraska Act) towards a position where he embraced black equality. Eric Foner's brilliant study of Lincoln and slavery essentially makes this case, albeit in a highly nuanced way. Michael Burlingame also thinks that Lincoln evolved from a 'mere' politician into a 'statesman'. 'Like a butterfly hatching from a caterpillar's chrysalis,' Burlingame writes, 'the partisan warrior of the 1830s and 1840s was transformed into a statesman.' Burlingame argues that Lincoln's support for colonisation of African Americans was merely 'tactical', by which he means that Lincoln publicly endorsed the idea while not really believing in it.[93] I think Lincoln's views of slavery and the practical legal position of black people in America shifted in the face of events, but it was more characterised by consistency than transformation. On the spectrum of antislavery politics he was more radical than most of his contemporaries in Illinois, but he was still a natural ameliorator – a gradual reformer by instinct who felt compelled by circumstance to take more drastic action.

This relates to the second claim – more implicit than explicit in the literature but no less influential for that – which is that Lincoln's nationalism was morally admirable. This is because in Lincoln's mind the nation was important only as the means of advancing liberty and human equality. I do not doubt that Lincoln thought this, but I confess to being sceptical that he was right. Without a doubt, the Union victory brought immense benefits to the millions of enslaved people who were liberated (despite, in the decades to come, being denied equality in the Jim Crow South). The triumph of the Union was an inspiration to campaigners for more democracy in Britain, and often cited in the run-up to the 1867 Reform Act which, for the first time, gave the vote to some working men. However, the American Union was not, even in the 1860s, as uniquely synonymous with democracy as Lincoln assumed – and even if it had been, secession need not in itself have made the Union a less powerful symbol of democracy. Indeed, as some abolitionists at the time pointed out, by divesting itself of its slave-owning states, the Union would have appeared an even more powerful advocate of the idea of self-rule. The decision to preserve the Union through the use of violence on a massive scale may not have seemed like a real choice to Lincoln since for him the Union – in its full territorial integrity – was non-negotiable. Noble ends and violent means – it is a more ambiguous legacy than his present-day celebrators acknowledge.

It is possible that the massive scholarly production of works on Lincoln, at a rate that has escalated in the twenty-first century, has obscured why he really mattered. By emphasising his unique qualities, we may have forgotten that the things he said and did were mostly the things that others said and did around him. What we learn about Lincoln tells us more, I believe, about Lincoln's world than it does about him. In an age of romantic nationalism, he, like everyone around him, related to his country in an intimate way, personifying it as having a birth and a set of ideals, needing protection and deserving sacrifice. Growing up among common people at the start of the

Industrial Revolution, he was deeply conscious of the ways in which he had bettered himself not just through his own heroic efforts but because he lived at a time and in a place where it was possible for him to do so.

Generations of Lincoln biographers have pledged not to put him on a pedestal, yet somehow there he remains. Perhaps he needs to be on a higher plane because he performs a particular function in modern American culture, embodying a set of seemingly unimpeachable values, setting a moral standard against which the rest of us can be measured. The function of historians is to try to make as clear as possible the complex patterns and interconnections across time and space that make up the world. We are contextualisers. And so all I have tried to do here, in a small way, is to explain as best I can how and why this peculiar, intelligent, articulate, in some ways brilliant, man made the choices he did and why they led him into the centre of a maelstrom of events that reverberate to this day.

Notes

Abbreviations

CW   Basler, Roy P. (ed.), *The Collected Works of Abraham Lincoln*, 8 vols (Rutgers University Press, 1953); online at http://quod.lib.umich.edu/l/lincoln/.

HI   Wilson, Douglas L. & Davis, Rodney O., *Herndon's Informants: Letters, Interviews and Statements about Abraham Lincoln* (University of Illinois Press, 1998).

MBAL   Burlingame, Michael, *Abraham Lincoln: A Life*, 2 vols (John Hopkins University Press, 2009).

RW   Fehrenbacher, Don E. & Fehrenbacher, Virginia, *Recollected Words of Abraham Lincoln* (Stanford University Press, 1996).

1   *New York World*, 7 February 1909.
2   *CW*, Vol. 7, p. 19.
3   *CW*, Vol. 5, p. 537.
4   *HI*, p. 185.
5   *RW*, p. 503.
6   *CW*, Vol. 2, pp. 96–7.
7   *RW*, p. 252.
8   *Reynolds's Newspaper*, 2 October 1881.
9   *Carlisle Express*, 1 May 1865.
10 *CW*, Vol. 3, p. 511.
11 *HI*, p. 57.
12 *MBAL*, Vol. 1, p. 42.

13 *CW*, Vol. 1, p. 8.

14 *HI*, p. 459.

15 *HI*, p. 202.

16 *HI*, p. 386.

17 *CW*, Vol. 3, p. 512.

18 *RW*, p. 252.

19 *HI*, p. 384.

20 *RW*, p. 252.

21 *CW*, Vol. 1, pp. 8–9.

22 *HI*, p. 114.

23 *CW*, Vol. 4, p. 121.

24 *CW*, Vol. 4, p. 438.

25 *CW*, Vol. 1, p. 8.

26 *HI*, p. 107.

27 *HI*, p. 499.

28 *HI*, p. 499.

29 *CW*, Vol. 3, p. 29.

30 *HI*, p. 37.

31 *HI*, p. 392.

32 Quoted in Shenk, Joshua Wolf, *Lincoln's Melancholy: How Depression Challenged a President and Fuelled His Greatness* (Houghton Mifflin, 2005), p. 4.

33 Sandburg, Carl, *Abraham Lincoln: The Prairie Years*, Vol. 1 (Harcourt, Brace, 1926), p. 140.

34 *CW*, Vol. 1, p. 229.

35 Herndon, William H., 'Analysis of the Character of Abraham Lincoln' (Lecture of 26 December 1865), *Abraham Lincoln Quarterly*, Vol. 1, Issue 8 (December 1941), p. 410.

36 *MBAL*, Vol. 1, p. 201.

37 *HI*, p. 63.

38 *CW*, Vol. 1, p. 109.

39 Thomas Jefferson to John Holmes, 22 April 1820, in the
    Thomas Jefferson Papers, Library of Congress, http://
    memory.loc.gov/ammem/collections/jefferson_papers/.

40 *CW*, Vol. 1, p. 75.

41 *CW*, Vol. 2, p. 320.

42 *CW*, Vol. 1, p. 260.

43 *CW*, Vol. 2, p. 383.

44 *HI*, p. 64.

45 *CW*, Vol. 2, p. 461.

46 *CW*, Vol. 2, p. 276.

47 *CW*, Vol. 2, p. 276.

48 *Putnam's Magazine*, March 1909.

49 *Atlantic Monthly*, Vol. 1 (1857), pp. 22–46.

50 *CW*, Vol. 3, p. 315.

51 *CW*, Vol. 2, p. 461.

52 Foner, Eric, *Free Soil, Free Labor, Free Men: The Ideology
    of the Republican Party Before the Civil War* (Oxford
    University Press, 1970), p. 223.

53 *CW*, Vol. 4, p. 150.

54 *RW*, p. 438.

55 *CW*, Vol. 4, p. 268.

56 *CW*, Vol. 4, p. 426.

57 *CW*, Vol. 4, p. 430.

58 *CW*, Vol. 1, p. 510.

59 *RW*, p. 426.

60 *RW*, p. 211.

61 *CW*, Vol. 7, p. 476.

62 *RW*, p. 426.

63 *New York Tribune*, 7 July 1864.

64 *RW*, p. 458.

65 *CW*, Vol. 8, p. 333.

66 Douglass, Frederick, *Oration in Memory of Abraham*

Lincoln (St Louis, 1876), pp. 5, 10, 14.

67 *CW*, Vol. 2, pp. 222–3.

68 *CW*, Vol. 3, p. 146.

69 *CW*, Vol. 5, p. 421.

70 *CW*, Vol. 6, p. 30.

71 *CW*, Vol. 5, p. 318.

72 *RW*, p. 430.

73 *CW*, Vol. 4, p. 169.

74 *CW*, Vol. 7, p. 23.

75 *CW*, Vol. 4, p. 271.

76 *CW*, Vol. 3, p. 27.

77 *CW*, Vol. 4, p. 433.

78 *RW*, p. 194.

79 *MBAL*, Vol. 1, p. 360.

80 Blackett, Richard J. (ed.), *Thomas Morris Chester: Black Civil War Correspondent* (Louisiana State University Press, 1989), p. 297.

81 *HI*, p. 576.

82 *CW*, Vol. 1, p. 289.

83 *CW*, Vol. 7, p. 282.

84 Rable, George C., *God's Almost Chosen People: A Religious History of the American Civil War* (University of North Carolina Press, 2010), p. 356.

85 *CW*, Vol. 8, p. 333.

86 *CW*, Vol. 8, p. 356.

87 *CW*, Vol. 7, p. 535.

88 *New York World*, 7 February 1909.

89 *HI*, p. 332.

90 *HI*, p. 185.

91 Wilson, John, *Memories of a Labour Leader* (T. Fisher Unwin, 1910), pp. 173–4.

92 *CW*, Vol. 4, p. 438.

93 *MBAL*, 1: 376; 2: 234–5.

Timeline

1809	12 February: Born in Hardin County, Kentucky
1811	Family move to Knob Creek Farm, Kentucky
1815	Attends school for a few months
1816	Moves with his family to Pigeon Creek, Indiana
1818	Mother, Nancy Hanks Lincoln, dies
1819	Father, Thomas Lincoln, marries Sarah Bush Johnston
1828	Lincoln's sister, Sarah, dies in childbirth
1830	Lincoln family move to Macon County, Illinois
1831	Moves to New Salem
1832	Elected captain of militia company
1834	Elected to the Illinois state legislature
1835	Ann Rutledge dies
1836	Recieves law licence
1837	Moves to Springfield
1841	Temporarily breaks off engagement with Mary Todd
1842	Marries Mary Todd
1843	Son Robert born
1846	Son Eddie born; elected to US Congress
1847	Serves in US Congress
1849	Son Eddie dies
1850	Son Willie born
1853	Son Thomas ('Tad') born
1854	'Peoria Speech' condemns Kansas-Nebraska Act

1856	Becomes a leader of the Republican Party in Illinois
1858	Takes part in seven debates with Stephen A. Douglas
1860	6 November: Elected President
	20 December: South Carolina legislature votes for secession
1861	9 January–1 February: Secession of Mississippi, Florida, Alabama, Georgia, Louisiana and Texas
	4 March: Inaugurated President
	12–13 April: Bombardment and surrender of Fort Sumter
	17 April–20 May: Secession of Virginia, Arkansas, Tennessee and North Carolina
	21 July: Confederate victory at Battle of Bull Run
1862	24–25 April: New Orleans captured by Union forces
	22 September: Preliminary Emancipation Proclamation
1863	1 January: Issues Emancipation Proclamation
	1–3 July: Battle of Gettysburg
	19 November: Gettysburg Address
1864	April–August: General Ulysses S. Grant leads bloody Union advance through Virginia
	2 September: Atlanta falls to Union forces under General Sherman
	8 November: Re-elected President for a second term
1865	31 January: Thirteenth Amendment passed through House of Representatives
	9 April: Lee surrenders at Appomattox, effectively ending the war
	14 April: Shot in assassination attempt
	15 April: Dies as a result of the shooting

Further Reading

Burlingame, Michael, *The Inner World of Abraham Lincoln* (University of Illinois Press, 1994)

Carwardine, Richard, *Abraham Lincoln: A Life of Purpose and Power* (Knopf, 2006)

Carwardine, Richard & Sexton, Jay (eds), *The Global Lincoln* (Oxford University Press, 2011)

Clinton, Catherine, *Mrs Lincoln* (Harper, 2009)

Donald, David H., *Lincoln* (Simon & Schuster, 1995)

Faust, Drew Gilpin, *This Republic of Suffering: Death and the American Civil War* (Knopf, 2008)

Foner, Eric, *This Fiery Trial: Abraham Lincoln and American Slavery* (W.W. Norton, 2010)

Frederickson, George M., *Big Enough to Be Inconsistent: Abraham Lincoln Confronts Slavery and Race* (Harvard University Press, 2008)

Gienapp, William E., *Abraham Lincoln and Civil War America: A Biography* (Oxford University Press, 2002)

Magness, Philip & Page, Sebastian, *Colonization After Emancipation: Lincoln and the Movement for Black Resettlement* (University of Missouri Press, 2011)

Nicolay, John & Hay, John, *Abraham Lincoln: A History*, 10 vols (The Century Co., 1890)

Paludan, Phillip Shaw, *The Presidency of Abraham Lincoln* (University of Kansas Press, 1994)

Sandburg, Carl, *Abraham Lincoln: The Prairie Years*, 2 vols (Harcourt, Brace & Co., 1926)

Sandburg, Carl, *Abraham Lincoln: The War Years*, 4 vols
    (Harcourt, Brace & Co., 1939)

Shenk, Joshua Wolf, *Lincoln's Melancholy: How Depression
    Challenged a President and Fuelled his Greatness* (Houghton
    Mifflin, 2005)

Smith, Adam I.P., *The American Civil War* (Palgrave, 2007)

Striner, Richard, *Father Abraham: Lincoln's Relentless Struggle to
    End Slavery* (Oxford University Press, 2006)

Vorenberg, Michael, *Final Freedom: The Civil War, the Abolition
    of Slavery and the Thirteenth Amendment* (Cambridge
    University Press, 2001)

Wilson, Douglas L., *Honor's Voice: The Transformation of
    Abraham Lincoln* (Knopf, 1998)

Wilson, Douglas L., *Lincoln's Sword: The Presidency and the
    Power of Words* (Knopf, 2006)

Winger, Stewart, *Lincoln's Religion and Romantic Cultural
    Politics* (Northern Illinois University Press, 2003)

Web Links

http://memory.loc.gov/ammem/alhtml/malhome.html – The
Abraham Lincoln Papers at the Library of Congress
http://lincoln.lib.niu.edu/ – Abraham Lincoln Digitization
Project, Northern Illinois University
http://54th-mass.org/june-9-1863/ – 'Written in Glory: Letters
from the Soldiers and Officers of the 54th Massachusetts' (one
of the most prominent African American regiments)
http://valley.lib.virginia.edu/ – The Valley of the Shadow Project,
digital archive of sources from two Civil War communities
http://quod.lib.umich.edu/l/lincoln/ – The collected works of
Abraham Lincoln
http://hitchcock.itc.virginia.edu/Slavery/index.php – Images of
slavery from the University of Virginia